THE MU ENTREPRENEUR'S PLAYBOOK

THE MULTI-PASSIONATE ENTREPRENEUR'S PLAYBOOK

CREATE AN ONLINE BUSINESS YOU'LL LOVE IN 7 SIMPLE STEPS

By

JUANITA RENEE JONES

PRAISE FOR THE BOOK

Thought provoking with a humorous delivery!!!

"If you have been considering starting a business, but have no idea on how to get going.......then get this book!!

The author provides a guide for aspiring entrepreneurs on how to build operational discipline to your new or existing business. Her step by step delivery is engaging and will provide the reader with a solid foundation for their business."

--Walter Ingram

And she didn't disappoint. The book delivered the very things I was ...

"I was looking for advice as well as motivation to finally give my entrepreneurial self a chance. Then I saw that the author is 20+ year veteran project management consultant. I was certain she would deliver. And she didn't disappoint. The book delivered the very things I was searching for: advice and motivation. Great read!"

--Anna Mogan

This is a great book that not only gives methodical information

"This is a great book that not only gives methodical information, it is heart-centered. It has you examine what your heart truly desires and what your God given strengths are. This is a masterful recipe for any success in life."

--Christy Cote

MY MENTOR BOOK!!!

"I was CONSULTED, COACHED, REMINDED, HELPED and REVIVED by this book. It's like my little mentor full of bright ideas for a successful online business. It provides a considerable amount of pertinent information, details and even helpful questions contributing to your success. I am more than equipped and ready to take my business to the next level because of this book."

--Elsa Mendoza

Methodically build yourself a business that will suit your passions.

"If you are completely overwhelmed by all the possibilities in the internet world, this is the book for you! If the mention of funnels and algorithms, lead magnets and landing pages give you a headache, relax, breathe deeply and start reading - help has arrived!

The book is set out as a six-week plan to action the steps needed to set up your online business, with very helpful "massive action steps" in every chapter. The author shares her mistakes as well as her triumphs in an easy to read, easy replicate and to benefit from way.

This is a book you want to study with a notebook and a pencil in your hand, to methodically build yourself a business that will suit your passions."

--Louise VN Liebenberg

Establishing an Online Business Made Easy

"Jones gives very practical advice for entrepreneurs seeking the answers to setting up and being profitable from an online-business. I was overwhelmed by the information on the subject until I found this book. It condenses the maze of information available on the subject in an easy to digest way. You could spend years attempting to attain the mass of information and strategies available in this book. Great Read!"

--K. Menchion

Exactly the kick I needed to move forward!

""We have much work to do and need all hands deck," says the author Juanita. I can completely relate to that! But with so much work to do, and so many passions and ideas, where to start turning your mission into a profitable business doing good?

It doesn't matter how many passions you have, and how many different groups of people you like to serve, as long as you start doing something! Step by step she explains how.

The book guides us from discovering our 'why' to make a successful business serving the world. With practical 'massive action exercises' explained in detail she helps to bring your business to the next level. With a nice personal touch and examples of struggles and lessons learned from hers and others, it's a pleasant read which makes you feel like you're on the journey together.

I highly recommend this book to the aspiring entrepreneur as well as freelancers and entrepreneurs looking either start a business or bring their business forward. "Someday I'll have a successful business," starts when you've read this book! This book makes you instead of overwhelmed, excited to get started!"

--*Suzanne*

Wow, I have found treasure in this book!

"I wish this book existed before I start my business ventures as it would have saved me a lot of money and frustration! This book is different in that it gives you some very practical tools to get your business off the ground and be successful without having to spend money unnecessarily. I learned about the importance of creating a Facebook business page and how to do it! I am now motivated to recognise and use the multiple passions I have to serve others and make a decent income. I also like how the author shares her own experience, which are relevant to my own journey. I will be sure to follow the steps and refer to it again and again as I work on my online business!"

--Carole D

Practical and Up-to-the-minute

"Juanita R Jones' Multi-Passionate Entrepreneurs Playbook zips along in a conversational style that feels as if your best friend is giving you critical advice.

I like the long term approach she takes, the 'pro tips' and the reassurance that it's OK to move one step at a time and not become intimidated or overwhelmed by others' perceived achievements.

For those who find social media advertising intimidating, Juanita takes you by the hand and gently (though not too gently!) guides you to explore the best methods and platforms to promote your particular business. Emerging and up-to-the-minute social media trends are also discussed.

Juanita's references and recommendations to further develop one's knowledge of growing a successful online business are a welcome addition.

Helpful summaries ensure you stay on track and her frequent, MASSIVE ACTION EXERCISEs help ensure you put what you learn into practice.

Excellent, easy to read, short book that gives you enough to help you get going but not so much that you feel overwhelmed or don't know where to start."

-- Stephanie Philp

Finally! A Book That "Gets Me"

"Finally! A book about taking my business online that "gets me". Before reading Juanita Renee Jones' book, I had read many other books, attended webinars, signed up for courses, etc. They all said some version of the same thing...find your passion, or find your niche. I have always been a person who has varied interests and multiple passions. Before "The Multi-Passionate Entrepreneur's Playbook", I was beginning to wonder if maybe something was wrong with me. Why can't I pick just one thing?

While reading this book, I felt like Juanita was right there with me—engaging me in a conversation. She gives solid strategic advice for getting your business online—what to do and what to avoid—all while letting you know she's been there and she understands the struggle. Her style is extremely down-to-earth and I felt validated and understood while at the same time challenged to take my business to the next level.

I highly recommend this as a must-read for anyone who is looking to start or scale a business online."

--Julius Campbell

DOWNLOAD THE AUDIOBOOK FREE!

READ THIS FIRST

Just to say thank you for buying my book and deciding to pursue your passions, I would like to give you the Audiobook version 100% Free!

TO REQUEST YOUR FREE COPY, GO TO:

http://www.juanitareneejones.com/books/audiobook

ACKNOWLEDGMENTS

Thank you to my amazing family for always showing me love and encouragement. Even when you didn't understand why I couldn't just get a real job and stay for 30 years, I love you, and I'm grateful.

To the committed online entrepreneurs whom I met on this journey, you rock! Thanks for being there and not letting me quit.

A special shout-out to the best accountability partners I know: (Big Momma) Arlene Battishill, best-selling author and Facebook marketing guru, Los Angeles, California; and (Sunny) Synnove Hjorthol-Gandara, career & life coach and copywriter, Hudson Valley, New York.

Without Self-Publishing School and the phenomenal community of writers, my book would not exist.

Katie Chambers, Professional Editor
Catherine Turner, Professional Proofreader
Mariah Sinclair, Professional Book Cover Designer

DEDICATION

This book is dedicated to the multi-passionate entrepreneurs who risk the safety of their personal comfort zone to make their lives better.

Whatever your gifts, talents, or passions, I encourage you to find your place of gratitude within and embrace the fullness of you. From gratitude flows all real meaning and success.

Know that your destiny is calling, and the world needs you to answer. I'm inspired by all of you!

TABLE OF CONTENTS

INTRODUCTION

LET YOUR FREAK FLAG FLY!

*"Service to others is the rent you pay
for your room here on earth."*
Muhammad Ali

Where this all started

Downsized. I know, it happens to many people. Then it was my turn. I had a great position doing work I was proud of and then no more. After a 20-year career in multiple roles, you'd think I'd be used to transition. I had my dream job in my industry. Leaving it behind was difficult. Although that departure was tough, later on, it would be the best thing that ever happened.

The first few days of the transition were surreal. My mind was spinning, reciting what just happened. I couldn't quite get into the new groove of not needing to drag myself to bed and out in the morning. My mind was a ball of furious energy with no place to go. After about two weeks of this, a new weight arrived.

My confidence had eroded, and I was self-isolating. It's still tough to think about it even now, and it's been almost three years. I fell into months of total depression and anxiety, fearing the unknown future. I didn't get out of bed; I didn't talk to anyone. Instead, I binged on television and comfort food of all sorts. It was the best of times and the worst of times for sure.

Now you might think, well, you've had 20 years of experience, so you're an expert in *something*, why not just do that thing? Well, after such a long career, I no longer wanted to do just one thing. I wanted to feel fresh and relevant again. I went from Wonder Woman to Invisible Woman.

To compound the matter, I'm also an admitted multi-passionate person who can't choose one of anything. I have multiple degrees, professional credentials, licenses, hobbies, favorite foods, favorite colors—you name it—all in the name of intellectual curiosity and a thirst for learning. So choosing one thing doesn't float my boat. It handcuffs me, and I'm paralyzed with indecision, which triggers feelings of depression.

A purpose with a view

After a few more weeks passed, I got a call from a colleague who asked for my help with a big project she had just won. It wasn't work I had done before, so I was a little uneasy. In fact, I had hired vendors to do it for me in my former work. However, I knew enough about it.

This colleague had become a friend, so I felt compelled and agreed to help out. My reluctance wasn't out of ego; it was out of fear. I didn't want to fail and let my friend down; plus, I was already living every day consumed with the constant examination of my "failures."

But I got up, jumped in, learned the ropes, and put together a stellar process to manage the work. This was a real boost to my confidence, and, little by little, I reflected on my prior successes. Things were turning around. The reason for this divine intervention was becoming clear.

Turns out that the work was all about connecting me with people who needed my help, lots of them. Everything I had learned and done over my career was available now to help these folks. It was a real win-win because I needed to be of value. I needed to remember I was and am blessed with a multitude of gifts and talents I've cultivated over the last two plus decades. Yes, I got gifts!

Learning fast & burning cash

Now it was time to go put those gifts to work and impact more lives on a basic level, an economic level. I knew it was what I needed to be doing with my life, but I wasn't quite sure how to get from here to there. So I did what I've always done: I studied. Social entrepreneurship, online business start-ups, internet marketing, and how to perhaps bridge them together to create mass impact.

The pursuit of knowledge along these lines was fast and furious, daunting and draining. Draining my mind, body, and bank account. For weeks, I was up night after night, making impulse purchases at 3 a.m. and still looking for the next piece of the puzzle when I woke up. Sometimes forgetting I'd bought the so-called answer to all my problems just a few hours earlier. Sometimes I also forgot to open it until a few weeks later. Has this ever happened to you? It's a common thread among online entrepreneurs, almost a rite of passage.

It's an incredibly seductive and long train wreck you don't see coming until your credit card limit has been nearly reached. Once that happens, then it's just sad and depressing. No more secret thrills. No more getting high on the buy. Nope. Back to the reality of life.

The reality is when you are taking on something this big for a while it is going to be uncomfortable. You've got to put on a new pair of shoes and take a long walk down an unknown road. You can either take the gravel road and do it completely on your own or take the paved road and learn from those who went before. No real right or wrong here, just a decision to make. No matter the road you choose, put on the shoes and start walking into your destiny.

What you will learn from this book

It is my aim with this book to help you avoid money traps and more common pitfalls of this business. I've become an involuntary expert in a few of these areas of failure, but I hope you can learn from my mistakes. I will cover not only where I fell but also when I made progress inch by inch and a few lessons learned.

I'll also share other entrepreneur stories either directly or indirectly. Through this book, you will learn a clear-cut path to creating your online business and marketing it in an affordable and systematic way.

As I'm sure you've already noticed, there is a myriad of books and blog articles on the broad topic of creating an online business along with many subsets of the topic including internet marketing, list building, or sales funnels. They each have something to offer the reader. There's value in it all. There isn't any original advice left, and that is not my goal here. However, every voice should be heard by the people destined to receive the message from that voice.

I will teach you the unsexy stuff about launching an online business. This book is not a promise to show you how to become a 7-figure business in 90 days. Yeah, I took that course too, but I'm about 6 figures shy of 7 figures and still to this day feel robbed by that so-called guru. It's also important to know there is not just one way to do this, which is why you can and should acquire many books about the topics that interest you.

Exposure to multiple viewpoints will help better inform your thinking. This will make it easier to develop your own voice, your path, and the roadmap to your specific success. There are many avenues to success and each entrepreneur must define his or her own. I hope that by sharing my experiences and knowledge in this book, I will help you reach your destination a little smarter and sooner.

The objective of this book is to show you step by step how to set up your professional service business or any other ideal business you want online. Once you walk through this journey, you will have done what seemed impossible before: obtaining the freedom to go after the lifestyle you seek. This journey will help you create your launchpad to that freedom.

Starting my own online business

After the work transition I mentioned earlier, it was clear to me that I needed a way to create a retirement lifestyle on my own and soon. I decided that in order to reach more people with my gifts, I needed to take my local consulting business into the online world. This would be my path to a lifestyle full of freedom.

For months and months, I tried figuring out what to do and how to do it in a way that makes sense for my business in the online space. I'm sure you have come across those great offers from marketers of all stripes saying they can show you how to make your first 5 figures in a week.

I bought the high-end programs, coaches, software, and all types of products from free to gee-that's-a-lot-of-money. I bought it all, but after my first year and even after spending 5 figures, I still didn't have a real business. Real businesses earn revenue.

Like most others in this situation, I wanted to throw my hands up. I didn't have the choice to walk away and say, "Oh well, online business just doesn't work." I needed to make that money back, and I didn't want to ditch my dreams of working untethered to location and becoming financially free in lifestyle and the pursuit thereof.

So I kept moving forward, and I regrouped. I took a look at all the products I'd purchased over the past year, and then I organized and categorized them by topic to see where it all fit in a business plan, charting out a basic plan and the marketing pieces necessary to grow a business. My first cash goal was to completely repay all of the money I've put into the venture. After that, simple world domination.

I looked for fuller explanations about how to start a business online. While there is a ton of information on Google search to answer that question, upon closer inspection I noticed that much of the information was an inducement to some other product or service on the provider's website. Now, I have no problem with that, it makes sense for businesses to be marketing and enticing even while providing free value.

But there didn't seem to be a real clear process detailed in a product without a heavy-handed pitch for other products. So I started journaling and organizing the various products and services I came across, information from webinars I sat through, and books I read, etc.

I also noticed in the many Facebook groups I participated in, everyone had questions about the various pieces of the puzzle, and most without understanding the three steps they should have taken before their current step. For instance, spending time and money on how to create Facebook ads before even having a clear audience and a product to market. Yep, I did that one too along with everyone else. Something about learning to create Facebook ads is addictive. Just the thought of cracking the code makes you think you will be able to wake the dead.

Just thinking about finally having this power in your hands is blissful. Your innards start stirring, and you can taste the sensation of creating money with emails from your hammock on the beaches of Costa Rica (insert your dream location here). This euphoria projection is the number one factor controlling our purchase behavior, once money is not an object.

After all the spending, I wish I had had someone there who could have poured a bucket of cold water on me during those first experiences. Someone to help sober up my purchase behavior. Realizing that you might also need that help, I'll take a tangent moment here to give you a four-step plan of action specifically to deal with this magic-pill buying problem.

Here are four questions to evaluate any opportunity or major purchase for your business, ensuring measurable success in this common problem area of the buying frenzy.

1. Ask yourself, "Do I know where I am in my business and what I need as the next step to move forward in revenue goals?"
2. "Is this exact offer going to take my business to the next level? Is it a nice to have or a need to have?"
3. "Will I commit the time needed to implement all of the steps of this new program without fail?"
4. "If I spend the time implementing it, will I earn all of the money back for this purchase before my next credit card bill arrives?"

If you can't answer yes to each of these questions, put the purchase on pause and go back to your business plan. Review it closely and make note of everything you've achieved in the past 30 days. Celebrate that achievement and every additional one. Regroup and focus on the next tasks toward earning revenue.

Test all purchases in this way before deciding on any offers, webinars, ads, sales pages, etc. When it's time to get a service or product specifically to move to the next level, you should know exactly what you are looking for and research the right fit in a trainer and their program or service.

I get it. Sometimes it's easier to look outside our business efforts to make us feel better about things. Especially for solopreneurs, it's tough to see your progress when you don't have a partner to pat you on the back. We want to avoid the heavy pressure of doing all the work on our own and sometimes buying new toys helps with avoidance.

But buying a new shiny object for the business (that you don't need) is like shopping for new underwear instead of just doing the laundry that's piled up for the last three weeks. It works for now and probably feels good too. But the laundry will still be there waiting for you to do it.

If you can't bring yourself to make the time to do it, maybe it would be better to hire a housekeeper for a day to deal with the issue, rather than spend more money to exacerbate the problem. Somebody will have to clean it up either way. Tangent over.

Why I wrote this book

After a year of research and implementation in my business, I created this book as a resource for anyone who needs to know from the outset the how to and why for on starting their online business, straight with no chaser. Although this book is intended to be a straight-line approach for what's essential to get right, it is not all encompassing. There are areas that I do not cover such as questions about legal structures or accounting practices that are best left to those professionals.

The book is organized to walk step by step through the most straightforward process of getting started. It is for those who may be new to online entrepreneurship but not new to business. The content in this book assumes you know business basics and have basic internet navigation skills. If you should have questions on something I cover, please feel free to email me.

The topics I cover are the best shortcuts and explanations on the subject I've found. I'm providing what I wish I'd had when I started, hoping it makes your journey easier and saves you time and money. Having the entire process laid out for you allows you to simply put it into action and get it done. It will save you time, stress, and the strain of figuring things out in pieces, and most of all it will save you money. Lots of money. Following this process, you can get your business online in less than 7 weeks.

Client testimonial

To illustrate how you can save money, here's a personal case study from my implementation coaching practice for an online business woman in the sales profession. One of my first coaching clients Cynthia, a sales strategist, was facing fear of going bankrupt and eviction from her home when I met her. She was overwhelmed and frustrated with all the courses she had taken to no avail in her business.

Cynthia was flushing money down the drain every day trying to make her business work. Six months into her business when I met her, Cynthia was savvy with selling and was friendly and likable. She was very gifted and could sell you the hat you were wearing on your head. She had several products at the time but no marketing strategy and was only piecing together the infrastructure of her business.

By this time, I had gained an incredible amount of knowledge from training with high-level internet gurus like Russell Brunson, Todd Brown, Amy Porterfield, Ryan Deiss, and Todd Herman, to name a few, and was ready to put some of it to work. After several conversations with her, we agreed on a bartering arrangement that would benefit us both. She would help me with sales confidence skills, and I would help her to develop a full-blown marketing strategy that would address her major concern of the moment. Cash Flow.

We got started, and I spent several hours with her fleshing out her business goals and how to develop her range of products and services. The goal was for her to know what to provide her customers from first contact throughout a long-term affiliation. Plotting out the customer and product relationship over the long term is also known as creating a value ladder—a concept I'll go more into later in chapter six.

Cynthia had products she was not monetizing to take advantage of the online world. She was a 25-year veteran outside saleswoman, so she had ingrained behaviors of needing to get up every day, pretty-up, and go outside to meet people, try to sell them products, and try to be an authentic version of herself at the same time.

With no real desire to be great at technology, she got by as best she could. She had hired a different consultant for every piece she tried implementing. Those bills were racking up while nothing was getting completed and no additional money was being made to fund that level of support. Something had to change.

That's where we began. In a matter of 14 days, I helped her to streamline her online operations by implementing a sales and marketing automation platform called ClickFunnels to reach more clients.

I created a profitable webinar for her mastermind continuity products using ClickFunnels, and I also helped her visualize and realize the missing monetization of her product offerings that had mass-market appeal for her audience of professional women. Helping her create a pattern of follow-up and follow-through on social media platforms, she tripled her email list in 14 days and increased her income by 200%. It was a wildly successful and fast-paced ride.

I was invigorated and loved being able to help her through this implementation service. I realized that given any online business I could use the same approach and produce even better results. The key: taking purposeful action with methodical urgency creates the rain makers.

Who is this book for?

This book works best with those business owners committed to winning and pushing through any doubts. They're ready to take massive action and need to move to turn things around. It's an intense process that produces better results in less than 30 days than you'd produce on your own in a year's time or more.

If you're reading this book and you are committed to creating an online business or you already have your business online but it's not producing the results you want, I encourage you to follow the entire process as I've laid it out in the rest of this book. Every day, every hour, every minute you delay is time lost with your friends and family and income lost for vacations, college tuition, that golden retirement, or maybe even the collapse of your business.

I urge you to clear your schedule for a day, get your new business journal and a few pens because you will want to take lots of notes. Follow this process step by step, and you will have implemented everything you need to set up and run your own wildly profitable online business doing exactly what you love to do. Now, let's go do it and remember to let your freak flag fly!

All the best!
-Juanita

CHAPTER ONE

START BY OPERATING IN YOUR GRACE

Mining Your Gifts & Finding Your Why
Week 1

"If it doesn't open, it's not your door."
Unknown

What it means to operate in your grace

If you had to think about it (and yes, you have to) what would you say is your best strength? Next, think about what is the main attribute or characteristic that people have always noticed, complimented, or maybe even criticized you for having? What trait or quality do you like most about yourself? Is there something that you find yourself doing for other people that makes you feel pretty amazing and true (some call this your authentic self)?

My natural curiosity, triggered when I'm exposed to new things, drives my fascination with learning. It's the way I engage with life. The way I "just do me." It's how I stop to smell the flowers. So teaching, leading, and learning are my primary gifts.

While my passions are many, there are, however, two central characteristics others attributed to me in my childhood and throughout my life: a studious individual always ready to learn new things, and bossy. Sounds like a great leader to me! I'll take that.

Whatever first came to your mind is likely your primary gift. Your God-given gift is uniquely assigned to you. Although you have other gifts and talents given to you, the ease of this particular gift is a measure of your grace for the gift. If you've been gifted the patience of Job, you can probably deal with small children and remain calm under fire with great ease. While those without that gift, would not be very graceful when put in the same position. You're given the grace necessary to effectively deploy your gifts. When you examine where you find that ease in your character for a gift or talent, you should start there to mine for your purpose.

If you're multi-passionate like me, you will undoubtedly discover a larger list of gifts and talents. You are probably a little resistant to thinking that you can name them all or give them a real ranking. I know, you love them all equally. I get it. If, however, you really want to move beyond that stagnation and get to a place of action, there is but one cure: take massive action. Dig deeper, make the lists, cull the lists, consolidate appropriately, and discern what themes emerge from what you discover.

After I reviewed all the things I've ever studied, tried, or had any continuing and consistent interest in, I drilled down to determine what I specifically enjoyed most about each gift at its essence. I came away with seeing that I have a grace for helping people with learning new information and lessening their anxiety and intimidation. I seek out that same interaction from every instructor I meet, and then transfer that giving energy to help put others at ease. I have a teaching gift and an empathy for people who may struggle with learning and applying new information: making me perfectly suited for my work as a consultant and coach.

Your life has seasons or stages, and each one brings something new for you to learn about yourself and how you serve other people in your life. You should look on it all with joy instead of stressing about connecting to one absolute thing. There are absolutely no absolutes.

Because I'm a coach now doesn't mean I am only a coach or need to always be a coach. I am free to operate in my grace for any and all of my gifts. That's the bonus for multi-passionate people. Our solutions are more robust as we bring a variety of skills to each problem: yielding better results and higher performance. The struggle comes when we consider the thoughts of others more than we consider our own. Once you get off that crazy ride and own the whole and all the parts of yourself, you can make magic in your life.

Finding your dream and your why

Having had many successes along with a few duds over my 20+ years in my career, I all of a sudden have found myself on the outside looking in. In the professional world, it seems the only women of interest are the young millennial women or on the opposite end of the spectrum, the baby boomer women. Being a Gen Xer, I'm wedged squarely between the two. Yes, one might also say we're pretty invisible as a group.

Now for my manly Gen X readers, I know you, of course, have issues as well. Whatever the symptoms are for you, just know that in spirit and in truth I get you. You're a bit hurt by the disappearing act that's going on in your life too. Whether it's the hair gone gray or just plain gone; or your kids have left the house, but you don't have any grandkids yet; or your career is over, and you've retired but want to get out of the house; or maybe you never quite got the breaks at work, and you hate your job, etc., there's something for everybody. There's even something for millennial men. How about these new 15- and 17-year-old internet millionaires? Talk about the competition expanding and running out of time. Ouch.

Regardless of the current issues in your personal and professional life, it is important to keep dreaming. So, What's Your Dream? Put another way, when you think about how you want to spend each day for the rest of your life, what are you hoping you can stop doing? For example, I dream about not having to stress over bills and being financially in a position to help my family. What about you? What gives you a sense of relief to let it go?

This examination is very useful as it frames the basis of the initial choices you need to make regarding discovering your why: your reason to get up every day and take action towards meeting your end goal. You will absolutely need this goal front and center in your brain and in your heart because every day you will be tested, some more than others.

And while, yes, we all want world peace, your why needs to be deeply personal to continue to drive your actions. The loftier it is, the easier it is to be less connected to it, especially when it's become a cliché causing people to roll their eyes. It should be strong enough that it is on your mind regularly, making it nearly impossible for you to be disconnected.

There will be issues that come up with family, work, technology, or financial worries that will deflect from the big goal. If you only have some faint notion of "it would be nice to have that," it won't take much for you to give up on your dream. It's all about the mindset here. When you're able to create the emotional connection and feeling of "I have to get this done before I die," you can achieve anything you want.

I know entrepreneurs for whom a very personal circumstance with their family members serves as their why. Some have devastating illness diagnoses, financial hardships, chronic underemployment or just less than satisfactory employment, need for a larger home due to an expanding family, or lack of college funds for kids, etc. These immediate needs are the basis of the active why: the why that motivates you to take massive action and make it happen now.

Once you get to the place where you've met all of those immediate goals, you can define a why based on creating greater impact in the world, your altruistic vision that will continue to drive your motivation in your business long after achieving financial success.

The passions of a multi-passionate

There's a lot of discussion today about the idea of passion. Pursuing your passion, finding your passion, what defines a passion, etc. Some of it is good conversation, but most of it is just good theater a distraction. Yes, you should love what you do and not just go through the motions. But many of us can take on multiple interests and do them each with fervor, and for us, this does not mean that one interest has more meaning than another or that one is the passion.

I do believe, however, that when we establish a connection to helping other people in anything that we do, the impact and gratification is so deeply satisfying that it surpasses the notion of one true passion which can be fleeting. Today it could be hot yoga and Zen meditation, but in a couple of years from now, it could be rain forest exploration retreats. Does that mean you can't do both, love both, and be good at both? So why then does it matter that you define your passion in such absolute terms before you can start a business that serves people in some way? The only thing that matters is that you start. The middle and the ending will happen naturally.

There's a great 12-minute TED talk on this topic by Emilie Wapnick about people with multiple interests and creative pursuits she calls Multipotentialites (but also known as polymaths, scanners, or Renaissance people). Certainly, if you only have one thing you do well that benefits others, then check this off your list. One and done. But for the millions of people who are multi-passionate and ever growing through a natural curiosity and giftedness, you absolutely cannot and should not try to force this situation.

To paraphrase Luke 12:48—from the King James Version of the Bible—To whom much is given much is required. So if you have more to share with the world, you must share more. It serves no one for us to withhold our gifts and not help others.

We have a serious and growing number of problems in this world. Much of them coming from our collective responses to the human condition on many levels, including how we process the emotions of fear and guilt leading to any number of now treatable-with-a-pill problems. I'll save this for another book, but you get the point. We have too much work to do and need all hands on deck.

Whatever it is that is firmly rooted within you to do, and that can help impact the life of another human being, it's time to man/woman up and do it. Slap a badge on it, and thy name shall be passion. When you find another awesome thing you can do to help someone else, do that too and call it passion #2.

Success will come from persistence. That persistence will meet with challenges all along the way, which means you must have a deeper connection to what drives you to be your best self in all circumstances and not worry about conforming to a norm of one passion per person. The connection must be *Built Ford Tough* as we say in the Midwest.

The goal of these massive action exercises in uncovering the why(s) and the gifts in your life is to clear your mental space. In this newly cleared space is where you can finally create an unflinching belief in yourself, enveloped by the best attitudes about yourself, that work together to make the conditions ripe for you to give yourself the permission to say yes to your own dreams.

MASSIVE ACTION EXERCISE:

- Go to your favorite quiet place and look back over your life starting with the earliest memory you can recall. Try to only focus your recall on the positive things and achievements no matter how small. This exercise is all about operating in gratitude. Recall those early memories like your first straight A report card in 1st grade or whatever your finest hour was. Don't judge it. Just give thanks for it. Then list it in your journal and continue to the next memory.

- Give thanks (to your higher power) who has always blessed you beyond your actions. Commit to taking massive action on behalf of the strengths you have to fix some problem you know other people have.

- Go out to where you might find people who need your help. Talk to three people to discover who you can help over this first week. Journal the entire experience and connect with how you were feeling while helping these folks. Write that down.

- Then think deeply for guidance on how to help more people with this gift of yours. Write down your first thoughts about the how. Save for later and begin to implement planning steps by talking to others in the field about how they got started. You will likely get your first client during this two-week period from just putting yourself out there and opening the doors. We will explore more on this in later chapters so stay committed.

NOTES:

_____

_____

_____

_____

_____

_____

_____

_____

_____

_____

_____

_____

_____

_____

CHAPTER TWO

SEARCH FOR THE PEOPLE YOU WANT TO ROOT FOR

Who are you meant to serve?
Week 2

"We treat our people like royalty. If you honor and serve the people who work for you, they will honor and serve you."
Mary Kay Ash

You need to get in the game

Over the past several years, online businesses along with social media users have exploded. For the first time in history, small-business owners now have access to one of the most affordable advertising platforms (Facebook) reaching billions of people. This access can bring about exponential growth for their brands and their customer base.

No matter what kind of professional service you offer— accountant, lawyer, financial planner, social media manager, roofer, contractor, business coach, internet marketer, you name it—there is an ever-expanding opportunity for businesses who serve other businesses.

The same explosion is happening if you serve consumers as well, such as a dentist, chiropractor, gym owner, yoga instructor, hair care professional, health/nutrition/life coach, realtors, and many others.

According to the US Census Bureau's report dated February 17, 2017, total e-commerce sales were estimated at $395 billion in revenue to the US economy in 2016, an increase of 15% from 2015. Forrester reports that by 2020 the industry will top $1 trillion. Thus, the time is now if you want to create a business in service to others while designing the life you've always wanted.

Who are your customers?

When you started building the foundation of your business idea, there was one ideal customer that came to mind. Think through the general demographics of that ideal customer and use your research to refine. Double down on what you uncovered in chapter one about your gifts and who it is you are best meant to serve at this point in your life.

Depending on your skill set and service or product, you will need to align your marketing with the end users, consumers, or businesses you can most help. If this is a new area of business for you and you have no data to analyze, just put yourself in the shoes of the person/business that you are designing products or services for. Reflect back on the people you met from the earlier exercise.

Follow the action plan from chapter one and talk to people you want to serve and get a real sense of their life right now. What do they want, and are you equipped to provide it? If not, can you get more specific training or apprentice with someone? Remember that developing an online business concept from thin air is like becoming an entrepreneurial mad scientist. Know that your first experiment won't be your forever thing, and that's just fine.

The first question you should ask is, "Who do I feel most qualified to help?" Think about it carefully because getting as dialed in as you can early on will make everything else you'll need to do to get in front of them a lot easier. Make sure your thoughts are not about degrees that qualify you, but that you have a knowledge base and experience that allows you to take people from they are to where they want to be. People in need are only interested in your ability to get them the results they want. No one cares about the degrees or even how long you've been doing what you do, as long as you can surely deliver the results you promise.

For some business owners, there's an emotional reason for the decisions made regarding who they will serve and with what solutions. I found my customer base through my experiences. My personal, professional, and emotional struggles, and subsequent resurgence from those struggles provides me insight into what may be happening to other professional women of my age. It's incredibly humbling to think about having a big impact on so many people who have been in my shoes or I in theirs. It's critical that you understand how your prospect sees the world as it forms the basis of how you will need to communicate with them.

Yes, this could be huge (said in my Trump voice), so you want to do it justice and put considerable thought into this step. The last thing you want is to make this investment only to discover in a year that you are working with clients who are not aligned with your value system and with whom you are not truly connecting. Phoning it in will not be enduring or endearing for that matter.

How to identify and find your customers

To start clearly identifying the client you want to serve, you first need to determine the general demographic profile of your ideal client. Whether this is a familiar market for you or not, consider using the robust Facebook advertising platform to determine the basic demographics of your ideal clients, based on your business niche.

The Facebook Audience Insights tool, found in the business manager account section of your profile page, has a tremendous amount of information on metrics like age, gender, marital status, income, interests, professions, employers, and even deeper insights on behaviors and usage patterns. The data is unmatched for volume and accessibility all in one tool, and it's currently free for advertisers.

The Audience Insights tool on behaviors is where you look to reveal specifics about the client's values or their psychographic profile. The discussion around personality, values, and attitudes is part of the broader marketing concept known as psychographics. *The Oxford Dictionary* defines psychographics as "the study and classification of people according to their attitudes, aspirations, and other psychological criteria, especially in market research." When trying to narrow down characteristics of your ideal customer, going beyond the classic demographic characteristics to look at these type of qualifiers is quite valuable.

Let's say that you've determined your ideal client is a woman, aged 35+, married, college educated with a household income over $100,000. This is a basic demographic profile, but we need to know more if we want to determine if this particular woman is also interested in starting a business, or needs a chiropractor, or wants to take courses in knitting or writing, for example. These interests are measured through data that Facebook has amassed within the behaviors and interests section of its advertising platform.

Lessons from e-commerce

The thing to note here is that no customer base is 100% monolithic. Groups are made up of connecting commonalities for sure. However, this does not preclude the group from having important differences within them. For instance, there is a huge market of pit bull lovers out there. Because I'm a woman and have an extreme fear of this breed of dog, I could easily believe (from my biased perspective) that women are not in the group of pit bull lovers. If I provided a market solution based on that belief without seeking out third-party data, I would be missing a huge opportunity because as it turns out, there is a large group of women who identify as pit bull moms and buy a tremendous amount of products for their dogs. Who knew?

Actually, Facebook knew. A simple review of audience insights for the USA, reveals that of the people aged 18+ with an interest in pit bulls, 61% of them are women with men being 39%. The largest age groups for both men and women are those between 18 and 34 years of age, with 44% married and 57% college educated. The top four locations for this group include Chicago, Houston, Los Angeles, and New York. As to spending priorities when measured controlling for buying pet products (meaning 100% of these folks buy pet products), 51 % of the audience spends on subscription services, 75% on food and drink, and 67% on clothing. Home and garden buying is at 18% and 29% for sports and outdoor activity.

You might be tempted to think that none of this other stuff matters, but that would be another miscalculation. If you decided to launch an e-commerce store, the pet niche is large with a tremendous amount of depth. As a sub-niche, the pit bull niche is full of rabid buyers as well. You could easily support a print-on-demand catalog with customizable mugs, t-shirts, posters, and hats, for instance. You could also create a convenient monthly subscription service specific to these owners, providing consumables they regularly purchase. The more you know about a particular set of customers the more you can target your product offerings for success.

When your product or service has a higher market price and requires more thought by the customer before making a purchase decision, this stuff still comes into play. You need to know the full picture of who your prospects are and what they value when your product or service offering is a high-ticket offer, such as consulting services.

You will know something about what they value based on where they spend their money and the locations they frequent. When considering how to communicate, what type of language to use, what type of incentives to provide, these other metrics make targeting even more effective, thus more valuable.

When you're able to provide more specific targeting, it becomes more economical to put your product in front of your best potential customers. This will dramatically increase sales because you're jumping in front of the best customer with exactly what you know they want, which generates more conversions (actual sales). Getting in front of the right customers allows you to reduce advertising costs by not wasting money on people who are not your targeted customer and who will not buy from you.

Three tactics and techniques to finding your Nemo

Next, you need to determine who your best prospects are and how they feel about the offers already on the market. There are a few techniques to finding these prospects, but you should leave no stone unturned when scouring the internet.

First, you need to know, like, and follow every group on Facebook and Instagram with a product or service similar to yours. This allows you to see what other interested parties are saying on a daily basis, what content they are reacting to with fervor, and what pain points they are complaining about the most. These are the insights you need for discovering new ways to get in front of a hot market demand that may not be well serviced.

Unfortunately, many people do not know what they want themselves; they often only know what they don't want. It will take some work on your part to get to the bottom of this. It's critical that you do because, without it, you can spin your wheels coming up with offers that are a total miss for your customers. You will always need to test and refine multiple offers with your audience until you find the perfect match.

Going deeper into the strategy of infiltrating Facebook groups can yield a treasure trove of information. People regularly post their frustrations about all manner of things in social forums making it pretty accessible and easy to spot. You can follow up directly with the poster and engage in conversation to get to the bottom of their issues, all without even mentioning you have a possible solution. You should just give value to the group by sharing some of what you know. You can do this in every group you become a member of and then position your offers on promo day (the day you're allowed to promote yourself) in a way that speaks to the larger concerns of the group based on your observation.

You can also start your own Facebook group and cultivate a fan base by serving value to the members on a regular basis. This approach has been extremely lucrative for many coaches and consultants although it requires a tremendous amount of work to get going and to maintain.

A second way to find your prospects is by looking at the keyword search volumes on the Google Keyword Planner site which is part of the Google business suite of products. The Google Keyword Planner allows you to enter a keyword related to your niche, product, or service, and it will provide you with instant analytics on how many people are searching for your keyword per month and also historically.

A third way to find your prospects and what they are looking for is through YouTube research. Because YouTube is a search engine, you can look for all the entries in the search box that result from entering your keyword or string of keywords such as how to find a good X (dentist, accountant, etc.). Once you find videos related to your niche, you can start looking at which ones get the highest views, comments, and subscriptions. This helps you see how hot your topic is or maybe is not. You also start to get insider information on what your competitors are offering and some sense of whether it's a winning offer.

After each of these attempts to discern what your customers want at this point, you will need to actually craft an offer and swing for the fences with your marketing. No matter how much research you do or even how much research has already been done, nothing defines winners or losers except sales. I've seen lucrative products with advertisements containing bad copy and graphics. I'm sure many have told the owner about the errors, but the sales speak louder. In the words of my favorite nutty professor, "No matter what, you've got to strut." Keep trying because you only need one. One winner, one big idea can remake your life.

Overcoming the doubt: stay the course

The only way to create a lot of sales is to make a lot of offers. It is widely acknowledged that the person with the most buy buttons online makes the most money. Think King Amazon.

However, it can be defeating when it takes offer after offer to find your audience, and this can lead to self-doubt. It's in those times that you need to stay connected to your why and focus on the greater impact you want to create. Even though there are many others who do what you want to do, you are uniquely attractive to the particular people you are meant to serve. Don't get caught up in comparing yourself to anyone else.

If you need a guide post for comparison, use the progress you make on a daily basis as the only reference point. This practice will help you stay properly grounded and stay the course. Because this online business is isolating and hard, it can be easier to just stop, and no one would be the wiser but you. The problem with quitting is that if you truly believe you've been gifted with an ability to help people and you don't do anything about it, you risk living a less than fulfilling life.

This happens all the time to many people you know. They give in and become complacent with being unhappy or some even depressed, deciding that they are not good enough because they couldn't push through the tough times. Don't give in. Stay focused. You are morally obligated to help the people you're meant to help, and you've already been given everything you need within to do so.

Everything else you'd want to add on such as certifications, degrees, courses, coaching, etc., is all just an attempt to fill up what you think are voids in the package. There are no voids that can't be filled by the experience of doing the work. Once you accept this reality, you can hold on to it to propel you through the rough patches. This does not mean you won't need to grow your knowledge, but the best learning happens when you are taking action.

In the recently released *Relaunch Your Life* by Scott Allan, he talks about learning from what doesn't work in your life, making changes along the way through self-reflection, and focusing on adjusting as needed since losing is a part of winning.

Allan says, "Instead of shooting for some gigantic achievement, focus on the next rung of the ladder. How many people do you know who can leap from the bottom rung to the top in a single bound? It's one step at a time." This is sage advice and particularly useful in strengthening your internal fortitude so that you're battle ready in creating a successful online business.

Now that I've been through an intense year immersed in training and online learning, I have a more in-depth understanding of why a Harvard study shows that statistically 96% of all online businesses close within four months of launching. That's a staggering figure, but I can completely understand why it happens. The real trick is to stay focused and just open a new one if you can't make the first one work. If you're not failing, you're not trying hard enough, and if you're not trying hard enough, you'll never win.

Once you zero in on who your ideal customer is and what they want, it will be easier to determine where they will more likely hang out so that you can get your message directly in front of them. For instance, people who are professionals searching for business information or help to move their careers or business along are more likely to be found on the LinkedIn platform.

LinkedIn is the preferred hangout for self-identified professionals and has a much more mature and business-like messaging vibe. You would be frowned upon and severely chastised for posting a sexy selfie or forbidden cat video. You'll find no excessively personal posts full of over sharing either. It's quite dreamy that way.

In the next chapter, we will take a deeper dive into the major players in today's social media platforms. I will walk you through the actual setup you need to do on Facebook and LinkedIn. If you already have accounts, feel free to skip the sections. There are, however, a few gold nuggets in the section for the LinkedIn profile.

MASSIVE ACTION EXERCISE:

Here are a few more questions you need to ask and answer to help you narrow the target on your ideal customer.

- Is your ideal customer a male or female? Knowing this will help you when crafting messages and using language generally most appropriate for the gender identified.
- Are they younger or older? What stage of life are they in right now?
- What problem or challenge does your product solve or lessen for them?
- How do they see themselves? What do they value and does it align with your values?
- Where do they primarily get their information (what sources)?

NOTES:

_____

_____

_____

_____

_____

_____

_____

_____

_____

The answers to these questions may lead you to other identifiers associated specifically with your ideal customer. It's important to make this connection early and to refine from here. Doing so will reduce the amount of friction between you, your service/product, and the customer.

You will begin serving the people with the attitude and values that you set out to help. This approach will ensure that building a long-term relationship is possible and mutually beneficial. In the next chapter, you'll learn about where they hang out on social media.

CHAPTER THREE

WHERE IN THE WORLD ARE MY PEOPLE?

The top social media platforms for service providers
Week 3

"You have been assigned this mountain to show others it can be moved."
Unknown

Now that you've identified your ideal customer, and you have built a psychographic profile on them, it should be much easier to determine where they spend their time online and in what they are most interested. The more you know about your prospects, the more effective you can be in helping them achieve their goals. Understanding their psychology helps you look through their eyes and tap into their perspectives on how they go about solving their problems.

This includes how they search the internet for answers, what keyword language they are prone to use, what information sources they are likely to reference, etc. Knowing which experts they follow is very helpful as well in acquiring a basic understanding of the prospect and what they want.

Getting to the next level of prospect engagement requires you, as the service provider, to have some imagination and the ability to think like your prospect would think. This gets tricky for some owners because they are fixated on where they are in the moment and what they need instead of where the prospect is and what the prospect needs.

As the owner, you need to know your marketplace and your competitors. Your prospects are reacting to the current marketplace and receiving information and forming opinions of the market based on the totality of what your competitors are presenting. This means that you should also be your competitor's customer, active in their groups, present on their news feeds and Instagram feeds, etc. Doing this will help you discover how to differentiate your services from your competitor based on the feedback from the marketplace of customers.

Infiltrating your market will reveal where your customers are hanging out. If you're in the Facebook groups and you see a ton of regular engagement or lots of posts on promo days, it means those business owners spend a good deal of time on Facebook, and they believe they are getting what they want. If you follow your competitors on Instagram and there's very little posting and no real engagement, that lets you know that they have an account merely to cover their bases, but they don't believe their customers are there. Same with all the other social media hangouts.

Generally speaking, Pinterest and Instagram are much better platforms for people in e-commerce, or bloggers offering products like their courses and coaching services to other bloggers, for example. Facebook is the best place to start for everyone because you have access to two billion people. If you can focus on the advertising platform with fierceness, because it can be daunting, that skill set is game changing for any business. LinkedIn is the platform for service providers serving other businesses or serving professionals. If your business is traditionally built on in-person networking type activities, you need to have a LinkedIn presence.

To know within a 99% level of assuredness where to find your particular customer, go to your competitors and follow the thought leaders in the space. When I decided to write this book, I searched the internet for "how to write and publish my first book." I found a number of sources of information and programs to review. With the tech savvy that is Facebook advertising, I was then retargeted by many of those advertisers as I went about my daily internet sleuthing.

All of this retargeting showed me ancillary products and services I didn't even think about like how to market your book, how to create a launch team, how to start a business from publishing your book, how to find the best editors and book designers, how to make money from Kindle, etc. So start your search, and the sign posts will find you.

Do this same type of thinking for your particular customers as well. You know a lot about them from earlier exercises, who they are and generally what they want. Following their leaders, so to speak, lets you narrow down where to find them on social media.

Now that you know the top platforms they hang out on, get yourself an account and profile on each of them and make sure they are professional and managed regularly. In the next section, I will cover exactly how to set up an account and profile on Facebook and LinkedIn.

While there are a growing number of social media platforms, this book will only take a deep dive in covering the top two most valuable to online business owners in professional services: Facebook and LinkedIn. Yes, there are plenty more including Periscope, Snapchat, Twitter, YouTube, Pinterest, and so on. I want to make sure that you get the most efficient start to your success as possible, so I'll only cover the platforms that have been shown to perform best in class for professional service business owners. Once your business is smoothly producing revenue, you need to be comfortable expanding into other areas; then and only then would I indulge in spending time and money on other platforms.

After reading this chapter, you should take massive action on at least one of the platforms discussed, and you can do it without shelling out any more to learn it than you've already invested in this book.

Over the course of the last year, I have shelled out thousands of dollars to learn this or that platform, tactic, tip, or trick. In the spirit of paying it forward, I've done the heavy lifting for you on this one, and I'm giving you the clear-cut best practices that will help you achieve the success you want in your business.

This chapter covers why to set up these pages and how. If you already know how or if you already have an account set up, you can skip this chapter. However, I do give some insight into how to craft a winning LinkedIn profile, so you may want to read that section. Later in the book, I will give you ideas on how to actually use these platforms for your gain.

I've organized the chapter to ensure that for each platform covered there is a full explanation as to the why, how, what, and where. The steps outlined are actionable to help you get going. That means you will be able to take this chapter, sit beside your computer, and follow along with each of the action steps.

Once complete, you will have a thorough understanding of the following basics: why to and how to create a Facebook Business Page (aka Fan Page), and why to and how to create a LinkedIn account. I will also provide a few Pro Tips that will help make things go faster.

The massive action steps for this chapter include setting up a Facebook Business Page and a LinkedIn account with a client attracting profile. You will need your journal and pens at the ready. Here we go!

MASSIVE ACTION EXERCISE: Create a Facebook Presence

Why do I need to be there you might ask? Only because Facebook as of this writing has over 1.86 billion monthly active users and 1.23 billion daily active users. It's safe to say that no matter who your customers are there's a 99% chance that enough of them are on Facebook for you to have a great online business.

Along those same lines, it's probable that you in fact already have a Facebook account for your personal use. If you don't have an account yet, take this book to your computer or smartphone and please follow these steps now.

Step 1: Go to Facebook.com and sign up for a free account.

Step 2: Enter your first and last name, mobile number or email address, create a password, select your gender, and enter your birth date.

Step 3: Click on Create Account. Done and Done!

And just because you were so diligent and business-like in your execution of that task, I am inviting you to join my free private Facebook group by going here https://www.facebook.com/groups/onlinebizhacker.

Drop in, introduce yourself and say hello to the group and let me know you took advantage of this offer of support through this book invitation.

NOTES:

_____

_____

_____

_____

_____

_____

_____

_____

_____

_____

_____

_____

_____

Why you need a business page

Now that we've squared that away, you will need to create your business page. A business page allows you to make your business visible in its own environment on Facebook where your customers can get valuable information and updates. This way you don't have to bombard your friends and family with posts about your business and have them comment that "Nobody cares, and you should get over yourself."

The business page allows Facebook users who may be searching to find you in search results. Also, you can now begin advertising, which is something you cannot do from your personal page. The main point of this page and your presence on Facebook is to advertise your business and grow it. Now, let's go to Facebook.com and set it up.

How to create your business page

Please note that there are a number of different routes to get to the same location on Facebook. I am using what I feel is the most direct route because it is how you already use your personal account by habit. My route takes you through the personal account page instead of the business section of Facebook. The business section is so chock full of information that you can easily get sidetracked looking at all these cool sounding articles.

Pro Tip: *Locate all of your digital files related to your business and put them in one folder on your desktop* *and name it something like "My Business Collateral." This should include at a minimum (where applicable); business incorporation papers, operating agreements, Federal tax ID paperwork, bank account paperwork and statements, any business insurance declaration page, business license(s), professional license(s), logo design files, professional headshots (or well-taken selfies with a professional background vibe).*

Step 1: Go to Facebook.com. Log into your personal Facebook account.

Step 2: Look in the blue title bar across the top of the page where the Facebook search bar is located. Look to the immediate right, and you should see a down arrow to click.

Step 3: Scan the menu dropdown box and select "Create Page."

Step 4: You will see six large icons representing page types that are currently available.

As of July 2017, that includes Local Business or Place; Company, Organization or Institution; Brand or Product; Artist Band or Public Figure; Entertainment; and Cause or Community.

Select the business type that best fits your company. If you're torn, just pick the one you feel represents you most. Favor that choice and make the selection.

Step 5: Click the arrow in the box to choose your category from the drop-down list.

Step 6: Underneath the category selection, enter the name of your company page.

Step 7: Accept the Facebook terms and agreement by **clicking Get Started**.
YES!! Your Facebook Business Page has just been created. Done and Done!

Next up, the new page will load, and now you can start completing all the relevant data inputs so people know what your company is about, who you are, where you are, how to contact you, and why they should care. You will want to keep this very simple. Don't overthink it. Don't think you need to run out and hire a bunch of people to get this done either. You're ready for this! This should take no more than 45 minutes for the newbie.

To make sure you don't create unnecessary posts on your new page, be sure not to click publish page until you've entered all of the information you want to enter.

You will want to complete the other input areas for your page. On the left sidebar, click on About and then click the pencil icon to edit each section: Enter date established, address, short description (155 characters), contact info (phone/email address/website), about your company, mission, and long description. Keep all of this stuff very simple. Short, sweet, and directly to the point.

Pro Tips.

- *There are many free design templates if you need more help in this area. Try Canva.com or PicMonkey.com.*

- *Click Add a Cover photo, and browse to your logo photo or whatever you want to display. The photo should be large enough to fit into 563 by 363 pixels which is what Facebook will automatically crop it into upon uploading. This is also the optimal mobile viewing size, and over 90% of all Facebook traffic is from mobile devices.*

- *Then add your gorgeous headshot photo as the profile picture on the left-hand side of the page. If you just set up your personal page, go back over to that page and add this photo to your profile there as well.*

- *Now for the professional service provider with years of experience, I know that you have a recognizable logo (icon symbol or text). Even if you've been thinking about freshening it up, resist the urge. **Use what you've already got to get what you want.***

- *Don't sweat the small stuff! Choosing a company type for your page, logo, and profile picture at this point is all small stuff. You can come back and change it after you've started making money.*

NOTES:

We will dive deeper into Facebook advertising—the good, the bad, the not so pretty, and the ugly—later in the book where I discuss online marketing strategies. If you just need to jump ahead, feel free.

Why you need a LinkedIn profile

According to LinkedIn, there are over 470 million professional users with an average income of over $80,000 a year, with 69% earning more than $60,000 per year. Over 74% are college graduates, over 2 million are C-level executives, and over 1.2 million are small-business owners. If you're in a business offering services to professionals, this platform is your virtual gold mine.

To maximize this opportunity, there are a few things you need to do to make sure you get set up right away. The first is setting up your profile. Most commonly people complete their LinkedIn profiles as though they are seeking employment. But when you are a business owner looking for clients and customers, you need a different approach for your profile section. Write your profile in a way that captures the attention quickly. It must say who you are or what you do for people, and then ask them to take some action to move the conversation forward.

One of the unique value propositions of the LinkedIn platform is the user's ability to grow connections by three degrees, meaning going from your immediate or known connections (1st degree) to their connections (2nd degree) to even connections of those connections (3rd degree). This extended reach is a main feature of the platform making it much easier to utilize in growing your prospecting base than the time and research you'd need to employ to get similar results on Facebook.

Additionally, LinkedIn has uniquely powerful and targeted search features built into the platform allowing you to drill down to exactly your ideal clients. Now that we know they're there, and that you can easily identify them through search, what is it you want to say to them once you have found them? This is where a well-crafted profile helps you stand out to future connections.

How to create your profile

Go to www.linkedin.com. Enter your first name, last name, email address and create a password. Click join now and follow the remaining setup prompts to create the account.

Important Note: Before you start entering your profile information on the site, make sure to turn off the privacy setting that sends automated notification of changes made on your profile to your connections until you're finished with all the updates. You do that by clicking on the profile tab (me), and in the drop down menu select **settings and privacy**. Then select the **privacy tab**. Scroll down and select **sharing profile edits** and change the setting to off. Once you've completed all of your edits turn this feature back on.

When updating your headline, which is the blurb area that shows right under your name on your profile snapshot, make sure to highlight what you do, who your ideal customer is, and the results you're able to deliver to them. Do this in an interesting and succinct manner to get attention and leave a favorable impression on the reader. Be sure to sprinkle in and use keywords for your industry so that other web searches might return your profile when people search for your service or that relate to your service.

Take some time to flesh this out because you have a limited number of characters for the section. Do all of this with the intention to attract those you want to serve, including when you accept connection invitations going forward. You also want to make sure that you include links to your website, blog pages, landing pages, etc., for people who are curious and want to see more. There is a section in the profile where you should enter the URLs for those sites.

Next, you'll want to update your summary section. Here is where you want to enter a basic pitch for your services. You need to say what you do for the target client, the results you've been able to achieve for others, how you're different from your competition, and how you want to engage further with anyone interested. Make sure to save the profile edits as you go along.

Finally, you'll want to enter into the experience section all prior assignments or jobs that speak to your credibility for doing what you're doing now. Ask for recommendations from people you supported or provided services to and make sure to get them entered on your profile. You're all set to begin growing your reach by leaps and bounds when you work this platform every day, engaging with your connections to stay top of mind.

NOTES:

CHAPTER FOUR

ARE YOU A DREAM MAKER?

Creating the right delivery method for the right product
Week 4

"If it doesn't challenge you, it won't change you."
Unknown

What shall I sell today, right? If you are anything like me, multi-passionate, forever multitasking, you simply have too many options to narrow it down. This is a blessing and a curse for sure. The overwhelming amount of information available on the internet is like a never-ending-everlasting-gob stopper (yes, Willy Wonka style) candy shop for people like me.

What do your customers want within your product or service?

After incorporating all of the research from the earlier steps, determining what service or product will best serve your audience is key to developing products that will engage the customer, increase your conversion rates, and improve customer satisfaction levels.

Your mission then is to get in front of your ideal customer and simply ask them a series of pointed questions to find out what they want and how to blend that with your best benefits. It's not quite as simple as saying "Hey, tell me what you want" because we are not often able to answer that question directly. The question itself causes a logjam of thoughts and paralyzes most people. You'll need to be a bit stealthier than that.

Try to use surveys to ask questions that will give you enough information to piece together exactly what their pain points are, and from there you can envision how *You* can best serve them on that quest for a solution, within the realm of what you are gifted to do. For example, if you're a gifted professional book editor, you may initially assume that your ideal customers are aspiring authors and lump them all into one bucket.

However, if you were to create and give an intake survey to your prospects, you might well discover that although you may be treating them as one homogenous group, like any other group, there are value differences among them as well. Homing in on the differences as much as the similarities can be quite valuable in growing your business.

This does not mean that the services you provide will change, not at all. The services can stay the exact same: copy editing for grammar and spelling, etc.; content or substantive editing for organization and flow of the argument; and developmental editing which includes content critique and feedback on a final product.

What changes is the positioning and the offering for each. Generically offering to edit one's manuscript puts the effort on par with a very secretarial, albeit technical, skill set. And as such, not much value will be attributed to that skill set as is customary in our society no matter what price you put on it. However, if you give a prospect three choices of what they want to get from working with you, the client will be more willing to pay the value you ascribe to each service.

Let's review an example survey sequence.

Question #1. Which statement below best describes you or your situation?

1. "I am a self-publishing author. I write exceptionally well, and I am only interested in someone to proofread my manuscript and nothing more."
2. "I am a self-publishing author, but I'd like my manuscript to be on par with traditionally published manuscripts once I'm finished. It's

important to me that my book reflects high quality industry standards."

3. "I'm a pretty good writer, but I want an editor to help me take my raw ideas, smooth out the structural flaws, and hone them into a brilliantly told story for the ages, setting me up for my run to best-seller status."

By the time you hit selection number 3, you could easily charge three times the value of the original offer without anyone flinching.

The point is to lead your customer down the path to where they can experience all of your greatness. It's better for you, and it's better for them. Your positioning of the offering does that for you. Based on what the prospect self-selects, you would send them to a new sales page in your sales funnel (more on this later) specifically written to address what they've indicated they are interested in getting from your service, and price it accordingly at each step.

The messaging idea is to appeal to the wants of the customer and blend it with the benefits of your services. You want to carefully position your value and tell your story, the benefits you can provide. This isn't any different from the positioning of a Cadillac vehicle over a Kia vehicle. Either car will do the job, but the positioning and the value ascribed by the manufacturer are what conditions the prospect to pay.

Taking this approach and adjusting your positioning, you could increase the revenue in your business three-fold overnight. Pretty good return on simple (yeah right, just kidding, artful is the word) copywriting!

Well known marketing expert, Ryan Levesque, created the Ask Method and has dramatically transformed many large and small businesses. As part of this method, he created a more extensive survey sequence asking a few initial questions to find out what people want. Then using the information to organize and segment the marketplace into three to five segments, he's able to help companies determine how to position their products based on that segmentation.

This part of his method includes deep dive surveys where you find out the language of your customer to put them in the right bucket and then follow-up surveys for those that didn't choose to buy the product offering.

The surveys allow you to gather information from people who are in your cold market (potential customers who have no knowledge of you) and your warm market (potential customers who have expressed a level of interest in you throughout your sales and marketing process but that haven't made the decision to buy yet). The follow up sequencing also helps you to dig into what might still be needed that you are not providing, giving you insights on what product development to explore next for your customers.

The Ask Method is a robust and intricate system covering everything from customer generation to traffic and optimization, tools and software, and an entire blueprint in an Ask Method Masterclass. It is definitely a blueprint you should review as you expand your knowledge base on all things marketing.

You are now at the point of the process where you need to go deep into reflection about how to take the gifts and passions you uncovered earlier and align them with your purpose—whether that's your financial freedom, creating an impact on the world, and or creating a legacy for your family's future. The Ask Method also addresses this component. Once aligned with your purpose, using the research on what your customers want, you can determine the best way for you to serve them.

Tried and true product delivery types

To get an idea of the various product types used in online marketing and to pick the one that will work best for your product or service, I'll explain the pros and cons of the typical models you'll find on the market today. So there's no confusion, the unique solution you have for your ideal customer needs to be presented or delivered to them in a vehicle or medium that will have the best chance of providing the impact they want and that you've promised.

It stands to reason that if you can't write, you will not make a positive impact on your customer through a blog—so don't start one. You might rock their world however through a well-executed YouTube channel video presentation. You must choose the vehicle to deliver your message in a way that suits who you are, your personality, and your internal strengths. Your message then stands a chance of really being heard and making the impact you seek.

These standard product types are formulaic and can be created in a number of industries. Some work better than others, but with minor tweaking, most models can work well. The typical online product models are electronic documents i.e. newsletters/reports/e-books, online courses (material is typically presented in either or both video and slide decks with voice-over), one-on-one coaching, group coaching, and membership sites. Let's review a few examples of each model.

Newsletters/Reports/E-books

One of the largest and most profitable publishing companies in the world is Agora Financial, a privately held company that services the financial industry. They are a half-billion-dollar operation with numerous newsletter subscription models that are profitable by serving hundreds of thousands of people.

Similarly, there are very profitable diet industry products like the 3-week diet where an e-book model forms the basis of the product, and then many diet supplements are offered as upsells throughout the product and the sales funnel. There's also a very lucrative affiliate model for this product.

Both examples show that products whose customers are accustomed to consuming a lot of technical information sell well through this model.

Great storytelling is needed to capture their attention and keep them engaged which is easily provided through the published document format. The products have continuity models (monthly subscriptions) with an average price point near $40 a month.

Online Courses

The most accessible and profitable is the online course model due to the scalability of pricing. The online learning industry alone is a $100-billion-dollar+ opportunity. This can be very profitable when all the pieces fall into place. It can also be a lot of work for too little reward if you want to impact many people but don't yet have successful marketing campaigns.

Growing a large group of raving fans is not as easy as it might sound. Even when you have a successful course launch and get a few students signed up, the success rates are daunting and can put a strain on future marketing due to limited case study opportunities and lack of social proof from former students.

The University of Pennsylvania Graduate School of Education conducted a study of a million students in online learning courses and they reported that on average only 50% of people who registered for a course even viewed the first lecture and only about 4% completed the courses. This means for continued growth of your platform, those in the 4% need to be stellar success stories for solid promotion and proof that your course works and provides the results you claim.

Otherwise, quitting your day job might take longer than you want. As Danny Iny says in his latest book *Teach and Grow Rich: Share Your Knowledge to Create Global Impact*, Freedom and Wealth, "It's not all entrepreneurial unicorns and rosebuds."

Iny is the founder of Mirasee, a business education company, and leader in course creation and coaching. The opportunity to teach and grow rich he says stands out in three important ways:

First, you don't need specific skills or resources to create your course, you just need to know more than your students and well enough to teach them.

Second, the market expands to reward many opportunities. It's open to anyone who cares about your topic, and people will pay a premium for education. This means that the opportunity exists for more people to succeed.

Third, online course creators can make an impact and empower others to shape their own lifestyles.

Mirasee conducted a survey in 2015 of online entrepreneurs polling about their efforts or desires to create online courses. Of those polled, 90.25% said they had considered creating a course, and over 34% had created a course. Mirasee followed up that survey with another in 2016; this time over 50% had created their first course.

Undoubtedly, many people will find great success in course creation. For all online entrepreneurs with a teachable skill, it's an important model to consider.

<u>One-on-One Coaching</u>
It's a simple model to start and comes with little additional overhead compared to any other model.

While this sounds terrific, meeting people and charming them to work with you one-on-one is where most people struggle. Working through the fear that comes along with telling someone you have all the answers is taxing and can shut you down.

Additionally, setting the price high enough to make all your time spent hand holding a client one-on-one worthwhile and finding those willing to pay that price can prove daunting. If the new coach doesn't have a strong mindset, they suffer tremendous self-doubt about their abilities to deliver and doubt their worth to charge.

They wind up undercharging, burning out, and soon giving up. It's difficult for newer coaches that want to coach on what's seen as "touchy feely" areas which are very hard to measure and convey value in dollars.

Because of the narrowing and hyper-niching down of their target market, it's difficult to create a marketing plan for growth. This creates a vacuum in marketing and tribe building in the off season of launching. It's a tough model and requires tenacity if this is what you feel strongest about pursuing. Where this model thrives is when you have become a sought after thought leader in your space and built a larger following.

Once you're that-guy or that-girl, and you're able to articulate with social proof how your students can make their dreams come true using your strategies, there will be those who want to get your personal advice enough to pay the handsome ransom of $5,000+ to sit at your feet.

Group Coaching
Then there are coaches who are able to make the pivot to the group coaching model and find it fits better in their lifestyle. Done well, group coaching is much more successful financially given the time commitment for the coach. In some programs, the students prosper more through the connections they make with the other students in the group.

High-performance coach, Todd Herman, has a wildly popular program called the 90 Day Year, which I participated in last year (2016). He regularly has multi-million dollar launches with this model and a highly successful group of students. Same for James Wedmore, Marie Forleo, and Michael Hyatt, to name just a few others.

The group coaching model can help grow your program and provide more evidence of your ability to create successful results for your clients. It also allows you to price the programs at a lower but reasonable price point that should boost your confidence.

Many group coaching programs offer a membership site as an upsell to the program. An online website houses information, resource documents, and videos, in most cases, and is accessible 24/7 by all paying members and updated regularly. The highest level group program is that of a Mastermind group where you pay more substantial fees to join and receive more personal coaching that speaks directly to tactics that increase business for the clients.

Creating products that your ideal prospect wants

Now that you've researched your ideal prospects and you're hanging out with them, you should be observing the type of language they're using to describe what's going on in their lives. You should be zeroing in on what their pain points are and what they are missing from the market. This intersection is the place from which you want to build your solution for them.

Continuing with the professional editor as our example, let's say she learns that the aspiring writers are expressing frustration that they lack the financial capacity to pay the typical $1,000 price tag for full developmental editing services. Maybe some are indicating that they want just copy editing, a more economical approach that gives them confidence that the end product will not have a lot of bad grammar and typos. Perhaps there are a good number of folks who are on their second book, and they self-edited the first and now realize that it was not a good idea.

To design products attractive to any of these authors, she would want to start categorizing the pain points she's discovered and crafting the intersecting benefits of her solution to remedy those pain points.

Depending on her goals and where she is in her business, it may be more important to her to have quality over quantity with clients. Perhaps she's a one-woman show, and only wants to do high-ticket projects.

Or, perhaps you need to increase revenue to your business and are not at the point where she can turn down proofread level work. One option would be to hire an affordable virtual assistant in your business to quickly handle simple jobs like this allowing her to provide a professional review with greater ease. The client benefits because the work is economically priced to suit them, high level, and more quickly completed because of the two-person review.

When constructing attractive products, you need to be able to express the benefits of transformation and results that your clients want. As you construct the message, your main goal should be to feed into their psyche that your solution will give them relief from a pain point or aid them in reaching the desired status. Once you reach this nirvana, selling becomes superfluous.

Once these clients become your raving fans, you can look at business growth opportunities expanding from editing to full support of the aspiring author who wants an author's career. This is where you plan out which of the product vehicles we discussed earlier would work for your lifestyle and personality while delivering the information or service to the client.

You'd have the option to develop information products and an online course that moves the client from a one-off book to that of a prolific author's career. You could add a membership site and then a mastermind group where you're working with them monthly on mindset exercises and scheduling, holding them accountable for production. Each of these products has a market value and can add significantly to your business's bottom line. Your messaging and its positioning is critical to meet both your needs and those of the prospect.

MASSIVE ACTION EXERCISE:

- When determining which product type you want to use to deliver your solution, consider your strengths: Writing/Blogging, Speaking, Video Presentations, Teaching, Coaching, Psychotherapy, Shopping/Buying products, etc.
- Rank these by your capacity and desire to do them. This will help you find a starting point for creating an online model to get your message out, which increases your chances of success.
- If you're a great writer, and you like organizing material and explaining concepts for consumption, then perhaps blogging or creating an online course is where you should begin.
- Even if you don't like writing, you can still create an online course by presenting all of your

messages via video training with minimal written material.

- If you want to stay incognito and just help people find the gifts they need to buy or items to bring them joy, maybe e-commerce is your jam.
- If you only want to talk to people in person, then maybe conducting live events or local coaching is your place to start.
- After ranking your strengths, select your product or service and use sequence surveys. Pay attention to the pain points of your ideal customer to further home in on your product or service.
- Spend a good amount of time researching the models mentioned in this chapter online and see what strikes your fancy. Write the positives and the negatives for each option as they impact you. Focus less on what the researcher has said that might be coming from a personal bias.
- Move toward the model you feel strongest about and then read on to learn how to craft messages to match your market and bring in customers.

NOTES:

NOTES:

_____

_____

_____

_____

_____

_____

_____

_____

_____

_____

_____

_____

_____

_____

_____

_____

_____

_____

NOTES:

CHAPTER FIVE

WHAT YOU TALKIN' BOUT, WILLIS!?

Are you speaking the language of your customers?
Week 5

"The life you live is more important than the words you speak."
Unknown

Now that you have identified your ideal prospect and where they are, and crafted your product to match what you think they want, you will need to start formalizing how to communicate with them. Your messages should instantly convey that your product is exactly what they want. Making this connection early and often is key to sustainable business growth online, and not doing it well is the downfall of most marketing campaigns. Typical messaging involves what the owner thinks is important about the product and shows no connection to what problem the buyer is really looking to solve.

Todd Brown of Marketing Funnel Automation, a marketing funnel expert and consultant to many of the biggest players in the internet marketing industry, offers several courses equivalent to a marketing degree in density and thoroughness.

His approach to marketing as a discipline is deeper than most on the internet. It's more academic: heavy on breaking down the fundamentals and gives a nod to the early masters who created the foundation that all internet marketers are using today. This includes even those marketers who do not understand what they're doing, where it comes from, or why.

We begin at the beginning

The beginning of direct response marketing initially happened in the US when Aaron Montgomery Ward launched a mail order product catalog for his mail order business in 1872. The big idea of the marketing strategy was to remove the middleman, reduce pricing, and go directly to the buyers for their response. Later, in 1967 the term "direct marketing" was coined by Lester Wunderman, the creator of the 1-800 number and other highly successful customer loyalty programs, and who is considered the father of contemporary direct marketing. (*Wikipedia*, accessed on July 30, 2017)

In general, direct response marketing is a form of marketing designed to extract a response from the consumer in a measurable way that can be tracked by the type of advertisement to which they respond. There are a number of delivery methods including internet, print, radio, television, mail, catalogs, telemarketing, etc. The boon of e-commerce on the internet and social media activity is rapidly changing how consumers make purchases. We are witnessing a dramatic shift in the retail sector with several historically large retailers deciding to shutter their brick and mortar operations because sales have shifted to online.

For the online entrepreneur, now is the next best time to get in the game and to understand how to create marketing messages that resonate with your ideal prospects and sell your products or services. Software solutions for getting out advertisements, processing sales, and tracking analytics are growing in sophistication and number, making it more accessible to non-marketers every day.

Now that you have your general product concepts in mind, you need to know where you stack up against the competition in your market space. First, see what solutions are already being offered to your prospects, and then you can start to determine how to stand out. There are certain key areas you want to examine when researching the competition including what language they use to grab the attention of the audience; how they express what the product will deliver; what proof they offer; what is unique about it; and what features, benefits, pricing, and types of incentives or bonuses they give, and any guarantees.

Taking these measures one by one and stacking them up against your product allows you to see any flaws in your product or in theirs. Once you've identified them, you have a new opportunity to fill the gap and make your product a true standout with some unique quality or positioning.

Example scenarios

For our professional editor, let's say that she has an editorial service that is generically open for anyone who might need editing assistance with any written material. Her service offering is pretty broad and general, a catchall for all buyers. This is a great way to start a company and test out elements before locking in on any specialties, especially because no additional costs are needed to do so.

When you first start any business, you're only taking a best guess as to what might be a winning idea. You will need data to support any real changes that are sure to produce a return on your investment in the company. That is where you start making your money back and seeing profits over and above what you've invested so far.

Let's say her business has now been operating for a few years; it's just breaking even and is basically an expensive hobby. The owner has decided she wants to grow the business to a level that allows her to leave her nine to five job and focus on what she's grown to most enjoy, serving book authors. She's done the previous exercises from this book and has a wealth of information to use in determining her next steps.

Her research has revealed that there are different categories of book authors who express their needs quite differently, so the target needs to be narrowed further. She's able to narrow to self-publishing authors because she wants to provide a compassionate place for them to come when going through the angst of trying to go from blank page to published author. She has a special affinity for helping people with that issue because of her own past struggles.

Now it's time to use this market information to create messages that will drive interested clients to her service. Having completed the product analysis mentioned earlier in this chapter, she should now take time to reflect on what these particular clients are actually feeling about themselves and their situation. How can she position her solution as a win-win?

From following the posts in several groups, she has gathered information to help craft her message:

- "I feel like a loser because I've had writer's block for over a year."

- "I can't seem to figure out what my character cares about, and I'm about to give up on this idea halfway in."
- "I'm at the finish line, and I've used Grammarly to help edit my book, but I'm not sure it's enough. I need advice but don't think I can afford a professional editor."
- "I can't understand why anyone who is self-publishing and on a budget would pay an editor $1,000, doesn't the editor crowd get this?"
- "I'm afraid I'm not really a writer, and my husband is right about me … I really want to prove him wrong!"

Using these samples as a guide, the intake survey discussed in chapter three, along with the other research on the demographic and psychographic profiles, etc., she can craft an initial message to start testing her product in the market. Her message should contain responses to many of these feelings by hitting on their wants and desires, their emotions and feelings, their beliefs about themselves, and how they self-identify.

When you're fully examining your client, you need to bridge any gaps between them, your product, and the market to come up with winning messages that will convert them into your raving fans and move them away from any competing messages or offers.

You need to make sure you are matching the market. To explain this, look at ads for weight loss. You won't need to look far to see ads with images of mirrored rooms, heavy exercise equipment, and half naked women with their rib cages on display. Setting aside the copy, the strong imagery of this ad would be most effective if shown to magazine editors who look for those type of images to sell their product.

However, when you're an affiliate marketer for the latest diet aid supplement, and the manufacturer of the supplement has positioned the product as the new silver bullet for women over 40, you're not matching the market with that messaging. Generally speaking, women over 40 are no longer trying to look like runway models.

They want something completely different and not superficial beauty. They want the aches and pains of aging to subside; they want their midsections to bloat less; they want more energy and vitality, to just feel good about themselves when they are around other people. These wants are miles away from being dressed scantily clad in front of mirrors and bench press machines.

At the end of the day in any messaging you produce, you'll need to connect to your prospects in a way that shows you genuinely care about them by getting them what they ultimately want. Once you do that, they will in return genuinely care about supporting you in your business. Your success becomes their success and vice versa.

Example from one of my failures

In my previous work as the managing director of a redevelopment authority, I had investors coming to meet with me concerning how to invest in the city without taking the financial beating they were experiencing. Feeling sure that I knew what these real estate investors needed, I worked on a product to suit their needs.

Due to my experience in the industry, I had specific insider knowledge to offer an informed opinion and provide valuable guidance. I conducted research on other products in the marketplace and found nothing exact although a few people were offering services to would-be developers/investors.

It seemed like a nice little niche product for the space, so I moved forward producing a lead magnet. A free checklist of something like the "Ten Secrets to blah blah blah." I put the lead magnet on my website, a sign-up box above the fold and in the footer, and I installed an exit pop. I had everything all set.

Then to drive traffic because I fully knew that people don't just magically find your website because you launched it, I posted a couple of articles on LinkedIn. I figured that's where I'd get the most traction because this was a professional services product meant for other professionals.

The articles received a solid number of views (nearly 300 combined), a few comments, and shares as well. The great thing about LinkedIn is they show your articles to all of your connections on their news feeds. From there, it continued to get traffic from shares and people looking for topical information on my article's subject. Ensuring that your post's subject and headline are timely, compelling, and even a little controversial helps boost interest for readers.

I examined the data for my website traffic and a good number of folks actually navigated to the landing page for the website from the articles which means I had a decent click-through rate. But no one signed up or asked for the free checklist. Not a one.

No one was magnetized by my magnet. It was so deflating after all of that work I'd put in. With no one taking me up on the magnet, I simply paused the larger product. I convinced myself that it was the only thing left to do. Just cut my losses and shift gears. It's only with hindsight that I now see I had taken the easy way back to that safe place: not believing in my unique value.

So that product didn't work out either. No, not because the market didn't respond but because I didn't have the fortitude to keep fighting for it until there was real evidence the market didn't want it. The lesson to learn from this is you can't give up after just one offer. It will take many offers to really dial in to what your audience wants.

I wrote two articles, and when they didn't come, I bailed. Quitter dressed up like a winner. The lack of response to my lead magnet felt like a personal failure. I became full of negative self-talk believing no one found me valuable anymore. Then I got crafty with it; I took the negativity to an even deeper level of crazy and decided that because I wasn't an investor myself, I couldn't play in this sandbox.

Digging for more and more reasons to layer on and convince yourself that you're a decided failure is the biggest waste of time and serves no one. As Henry Ford said, "If you think you can or you think you can't, you're right." So just decide already. Winner or Quitter; and you're not a quitter!

Sadly, turning on ourselves with a defeatist attitude is way more prevalent than you'd think. This thinking leads us down a rabbit hole, and many of us wind up giving up because the experience is painful. Most of us don't have a support system in place at the beginning, and that makes it even more difficult. You need someone near you who can give you a good slap to shake you back to your senses.

The great news is that it doesn't have to be a painful experience. If you can tell yourself to keep it simple and operate in a realistic fashion, success is there for the taking. Everything else that happens along the way is just part of the experience. More people will bail out than stick it out, so your odds just got that much better for greater success.

As I look back at all of this, I want to slap myself for allowing my flawed mindset to take me out of the game for over six months. It's incredible what your mind can do when you're not looking. I recently became aware of the term imposter syndrome. I'd never heard the term until learning more about online entrepreneurship. I didn't realize it was like the shingles virus, already inside you, lying in wait to flare up at the most inopportune time. Apparently, it's quite a thing, and I've got a good helping of it along with a ton of others.

Financial planner, Carl Richards, who wrote an article in the *New York Times* in October of 2015, "Learning to Deal with the Imposter Syndrome," said that "Two American psychologists, Pauline Clance and Suzanne Imes, gave it a name in 1978: the impostor syndrome."

They described it as a feeling of "phoniness in people who believe they are not intelligent, capable or creative despite evidence of high achievement." While these people "are highly motivated to achieve," they also "live in fear of being 'found out' or exposed as frauds."

Yes, it sounds all too familiar. But as Mr. Richards points out it is comforting to know you're not alone. Or as my business coach, Todd Herman, says often, "You're no special snowflake!" I'll discuss more about Coach Todd Herman in the chapter wrapping things up. It's a great part of the book, so don't skip it.

The point here is I bailed because I was seeking quick success, and I didn't get it. We often seek quick success without putting in the real work. I don't think it's intentional. I think we're just conditioned for poorly aligned thinking because we are inundated with all of these marketing messages about some guy's overnight success.

The real nutty part is that people replicate those messages and that hype because the hype sells. We eat it up and buy, buy, buy. All while there are voices of dissension saying it's not right; it's not what people want, yet people are still buying as a result of those messages.

With all of that said, the bottom line is converting your messages to buyers is a numbers game. The response rates for all of this are tiny when you think about it. Even though it's obvious that there are a few things I did wrong or out of order, had I used the numbers as a guide to make decisions on the next steps, I could have course corrected and worked my way into a better decision than taking my marbles and going home.

The Numbers Game

In April 2017, Constant Contact, one of the oldest and largest customer relationship management (CRM) providers (sending over 200 million emails a year for their customers), reported that their customers' open rate for emails in the consultant and training area was 14.73%. The click-through rate, meaning the rate at which readers took action in the email and clicked on a link, was at 7.35%. What this means is that 92.65% did NOT open the email and click through.

This is a major area of great tension for new entrepreneurs. We continue to think only in terms of what the gurus are quoting for their open rates without setting more realistic goals for our own business when just getting started.

Gurus say things like, "We're getting 50% conversions on our webinars when the average is only 10%," which is said to make you believe you will achieve these same results if you buy their product. We are more apt to buy because the extreme results are pervasively marketed, but they do not show the years struggling. Online entrepreneurship is a long-game play, not a Friday night lottery ticket.

Lessons learned from my failure

Let's examine my so-called pre-launch.

Reflecting back on the pre-launch, I can see where I went wrong.

- I had only written two articles. Ever.
- I had no following and no presence online before that, and I only published them on one platform, LinkedIn.
- I had made no outreach to realtor or investor groups, other social media platforms, or tried paid advertising for cold traffic generation, or anything I knew to do beyond what I did.

Kill the Deal

There's an approach we use in the real estate developer world we call "Kill the Deal." Meaning you throw every reason the deal won't work on a white board and solve for it until you can't solve anymore. If there's anything

THE MULTI-PASSIONATE ENTREPRENEUR'S PLAYBOOK

left that remains unsolvable, then and only then do you kill the deal and move on to the next.

Same thing applies in this online marketing world. You have to create offer after offer and dig deep on finding the ideal customer to make the beautiful connection you're after. After you've done all you know to do and they still won't come, then it's ok to bail and choose a new offer.

But by that time, if you're talking to your potential customers during the process, you will have a better clue what they want from you. That's then the product you give them.

This problem is typical of newbie online entrepreneurs. We're so worked up by the time we've put ourselves out there that if we aren't pleased with the results, or heaven forbid we hear crickets, we shut down and switch contexts to something else that will hurt a little less. At least for a little while. I think it's an unspoken part of the secret hazing of online business owners.

But you're not a quitter, so you march forward. You need to figure out which online business marketing strategy you want to deploy and own it. What medium are you best suited to slay and reach your customers? In the next chapter, I'll review the major online business marketing strategies to highlight differences and opportunities for success.

In the meantime, review the next massive action exercise to work on crafting a solid draft marketing message for your product or service. Back up this effort with the research on the client, where they hang out, and what language they are using in their posts to describe how they're feeling about the situation or themselves.

MASSIVE ACTION EXERCISE:

- In the last chapter exercise, you determined which online product types most appeal to you and will make the delivery of your product or service easiest for your ideal client. Go back into the groups where your people hang out and ask around about those type of products to find what your prospective clients enjoy. "Hey, what's the best online course you've ever taken and who is the instructor?" Or "What e-book inspired you?" Do this for each product type you're considering and do this in multiple groups where you've made connections and been active. Get the good, the bad, and the ugly. Most people love the opportunity to dish.

- Using the results, go directly to those instructors'/authors'/business owners' websites and start following them and studying how they communicate to the market, their branding, their newsletters, courses, etc. Start to use this information to measure your product concept against. Keep digging until you find a place where you can differentiate yourself and your product from theirs.

- Most important thing!!! Do not compare yourself to them. Do not think you need to have a $50,000 website and a team of 20 to sell your course. You do not. They sold their first courses from napkins. I don't know that for sure, but you get the idea. Take baby steps and keep stepping.
- Start to craft messages around your prospects' problems and tie them to your solution. Be honest and straight up with a little flourish for good measure.
- The end goal of this exercise section is for you to craft your first real messages about your product. You should get to the statements that clearly articulate the promise of your product, the benefits over others, and the other areas mentioned above as key for examining your competition.
- Write down the drafted statements. You will need these to grow from and later refine.

NOTES:

NOTES:

CHAPTER SIX

WE DOIN' BIZNESS HERE!

Online Business Marketing Strategies
Week 6

"Don't be intimidated by what you don't know. That can be your greatest strength and ensure that you do things differently from anyone else."
Sara Blakely

There are a good number of strategies out there, so it can be confusing and hard to figure out which ones you should invest in. You will want to invest in at least one of the top three time-tested online business marketing strategies in use today: (1) creating a blog or website to post and share your content for prospects to see, and optimizing those sites using search engine optimization (SEO) to grow your traffic more organically; (2) social media marketing and advertising; and (3) growing an email list of your audience members.

Creating a website and/or blog

I remember a time when having a website was a luxury item that only the big business crowd were able to afford. Then along came the free page by the email providers, and everyone was able to have a presence. These pages were mostly used as a photo album for long-distance family members.

Today having a website is the equivalent of having a business card, and in fact, it's replaced the business card for some businesses. There are now multi-page sophisticated business website templates available for free as part of buying a domain name and hosting package with any number of hosting companies, and they also have easy SEO applications to add on.

In my opinion, the business owner should not get bogged down in learning SEO. I'd pay for the web host add-on service and be done. With all of the changes in Google over the last few years, SEO has been marginalized and automated as much as you'd really need. SEO is a way for your traffic to organically find your website through search algorithms, and that's happening very differently now, so I'd not spend much time on this.

Just when it's a no-brainer to establish a web presence with a good-looking website, few people visit websites like we used to. We don't browse them for very long, or absorb tons of content. That puts pressure on the business owner to get the critical message on the front page of the site, above the fold of the page, and right in your face.

The whole point of a website or a blog is to get your messages out to find your audience. Health practitioners, social entrepreneurs, marketing educators, food specialists, etc., all need a vehicle to take their messages to their audience and provide the value they need. However, at the end of the day, it's no longer just a static website or blog page that will do the trick.

People today have no time or patience to interact like we used to online. We're staying on landing pages less than eight seconds, so the page/blogs need to get to the point, like ASAP. Not only do they need to get to the point, but they need to let the audience know that they have tremendous value to offer them to solve their problems.

This means the website has to be set up to meet your number one priority, which should be customer acquisition. This is simple to do if you only have one offer to make. If you have more than one offer, however, this gets to be a bit more difficult and techy. At least it did for me, and it was very time consuming as well. I realized that if I were going to offer my real estate investors a product and my wanna-be developers a coaching services program, I'd need a way to capture the attention of both with the one website.

To handle different offers, I'd need a new landing page related to each offer. So after spending three or four weeks trying to figure out how to get an audience to my website; changing the lead magnet, the site messaging, Leadpages, ConvertKit, etc. several times; and feeling the frustration, I started to get overwhelmed.

I started sinking into the negative thought pool that maybe I just couldn't do it. At a minimum, I had no clue *how* to do it. So, day after day, night after night, I'd look for solutions to this issue. How to have multiple offers and serve multiple people in my niche with multiple products.

One night around 3 a.m., I saw an ad for ClickFunnels that caught my eye. I had seen one of their ads before (the one with the husband and wife owners) but never had the inclination to listen all the way. This night I saw a new ad.

It was the cool video explainer ad that shows how it all connects with any type of business and how it's designed to help you make all the offers you want and serve as many people as you can. Boy oh boy was it a godsend at that moment.

This Russell Brunson (founder of ClickFunnels) dude had just solved all my problems in his sleep. Well, at least one of us was sleeping.

The ClickFunnels Etison Suite platform would do everything I needed to be done, and I'd only need to pay one vendor, know one password, and learn one new system.

And, I could create a business (sales & marketing funnel) for as many ideas as I could come up with. That last piece was the most exciting for a serial entrepreneur like me. It was very clear, ClickFunnels was a no-brainer, and it was free for 14 days. Sweet!

I fell in love with it. They were providing so much training on internet marketing it was unreal. I'd never seen so much value from a vendor in the space before.

Sure there was vendor training on how to use the software, or the template, or the email system, but not on how to create a successful online business that could help you change the world. That is Russell's unfair advantage among his competitors. Not only is he passionate about creating other entrepreneurs and seeing their lives change and the cycle repeated over and over, but his business makes his dream the reality for other entrepreneurs.

After all the research, I'm of the opinion that simple landing pages integrated into your sales and marketing funnels make the most sense, especially for solopreneurs. Whether or not you choose ClickFunnels is, of course, up to you, but I'm a fangirl! If you want to know whether it makes sense for you just email me.

Social media marketing

Trends in Social Media Advertising

Social media marketing is an ever-changing landscape, and it's important to recognize that this is due to the changing wants of the customers, the consumers of social media. As such, social media platforms will move to "improve" the platform in response to them, and this will acutely impact online businesses. Success is achievable for the nimble and quick. You can't really set it and forget it on these platforms.

Changes made over the last few years to Facebook feeds mean that a very small percentage of your posts are actually seen by your friends so you need to pay to expand your reach. Business owners are often just getting the hang of using these platforms to grow their business, and then suddenly the algorithm changes, and everything falls apart.

With Facebook, business owners will need to spend more money to stay in the advertising game on the platform or look for less expensive platforms. It will require more capital for investment by the small companies either way.

Just know this going in, and don't be fooled by the marketers telling you that Facebook ads are so easy and will make you millions overnight. Not happening.

In fact, as I write this, Facebook has been going through several mini changes to the advertising platform over the last couple of months, and many businesses, particularly in the e-commerce space, have been losing a lot of money while continuing to do business as usual with no guidance in place yet on the changes.

When your margins are razor thin to begin with, taking losses on Facebook ads can put you right out of business. This is why the e-commerce guy who shows you he "made" a million dollars on his Shopify store in the last four months is trying to sell you a course on how he did it for the low, low price of $997 today and increasing to $3,000 tomorrow. Although he may have pushed a million dollars in "product sales" for $5 fidget spinners through his site, his actual profit after all expenses is very low, say 10-20% if he's lucky, and since he gets 90%+ profit on the big-ticket courses, well, you do the math.

We know there are some big winners in the ads game. Sadly, there are many small businesses that can't compete and end up lost to the game. One way to best mitigate this loss is to diversify your advertising portfolio, but there are pros and cons on all sites.

Instagram, is in the midst of changing its algorithm as well. There's a recent phenomenon called "shadow banning" happening on Instagram and Twitter where accounts are being blocked or harmed in their engagement stats usually without their owners receiving notice of any issues.

In some cases, accounts are even being closed without notice, mostly due to a crackdown on fake accounts. This has thrown the use of automated systems to post and drive engagement into question and likely will change the course of those businesses dramatically.

In particular, Instagress and Mass Planner have recently had to close their doors due to this issue with account holders being banned by Instagram. It's critical to play by the rules and adhere to the terms of service for these platforms, or else you're risking the farm.

Instagram is a photo-centric social sharing platform that businesses have latched onto in order to expand brand reach into their customers' daily lives. Brands large and small have set up accounts and post photos relative to their products or services, and their customers become followers of their accounts. The platform is also advertiser friendly and more and more sponsored (paid) posts occur in the feeds.

The other great thing about Instagram is the relatively easy way to engage with other people and their content. I love that when you scroll, within your feed, you get a large photo without distraction from other content. Whatever you post is directly viewed up close and personal allowing you to hold the user's attention for much longer if the content is arresting.

For a long while, this was a phenomenal way to engage potential customers with your content, and you had the benefit of all of your followers seeing that content without paid advertising. But, that didn't last long. Recent changes in the Instagram algorithm mean it operates in the same way as Facebook, and only select people will see your posts through the system.

Amy Tori, contributor to the *HuffPost* recently wrote this article: "Dear Instagram, We Hate The Stupid Algorithm—Sincerely, Every User." The title says it all: long-time users do not welcome this new "improvement."

I'm hoping that somewhere there are a few big money players in their labs right now creating a fabulously game-changing platform specifically for business to business users without the need to suppress content sharing.

The fact is that these platforms recognize they are making a killing on the advertising side of the business, and now they seek to exploit it as much as possible. When they suppress free sharing of your content, it means you'll need to spend more to advertise and reach your same audience.

Only time will tell where this ends up. As a new or up-and-coming online entrepreneur, you just need to be armed with this information and get prepared with a plan of action. If you know that your audience hangs out on Instagram, that's where you need to be and buying exposure will be necessary. Here are a few tips for getting started.

MASSIVE ACTION EXERCISE:

Best Practices for Instagram Account Development

- Set up your profile. After you register your account, set the profile to a business profile.
- Enter a clear, catchy, and concise username; a description of your business; and a hyperlink to your landing page or website.
- Conduct some research on your niche audience and explore the popular hashtags they commonly use in their posts.
- Browse those hashtag feeds and follow the influencers.
- Once you follow the influencers, go into their followers and follow those profiles you like and whom you'd like to know more about.
- The typical response is they will follow you as well.
- Once you've built up several followers for the day, you can begin to unfollow those whom you're not interested in serving.
- Curate as much content as you can on a daily basis and bookmark it for posting a few items per day.
- Review your followers' posts while commenting and liking a few a day. This may seem simple, and it is. It is also, however, quite time consuming.

NOTES:

This need for more time-efficient methods saw the software industry create a solution called bots. Since bots are not actual humans liking, following, and posting, Instagram is calling foul on accounts that use them. It cheapens the engagement and social interactions of the real users.

The perceived value of the Instagram feed is all about the number of followers. Some gurus in the space have indicated you need to break the 10,000 mark of followers before trying to monetize the account. This likely works when you're selling items that have universal appeal: commodities like e-commerce products, e.g., Kendall Jenner's lip gloss.

For small-business owners to grow a business presence will require a significant investment of time and effort. One process for leveraging your brand involves paying influencers to promote you on their feeds. Through a "shout-out" practice where they send out a message to their followers introducing you, your product, or brand, the hope is that you get spin-off followers checking you out and, hopefully, clicking the link in your bio for whatever offer it is that you're promoting.

These social influencers are paid a fee to do those shout-outs, thus, monetizing their accounts. You can also go straight to the platform to place sponsored advertising that would be more targeted to your ideal customers. These ads are easily set up in your Facebook ads account which is where you create ads to run on Instagram.

As it stands now, the rates are still extremely competitive for the amount of reach you're able to get for the cost. This type of advertising must be part of your marketing arsenal if you want to diversify your options and build a sustainable marketing campaign year after year.

Facebook Advertising
Knowing how to place successful ads on Facebook has to be the most lucrative skill set in the world of internet marketing today. In fact, there's no shortage of online courses, programs, mentors, gurus, etc., all specifically focused on helping you advertise your business on Facebook. Success, however, is the elusive sleeping beauty.

Why is this important for my business, you might ask? Forbes reported in September 2016 that there were over 60 million active small-business pages on Facebook and 4 million of those businesses pay for social media advertising on Facebook.

The numbers continue to increase every day. If you want to do business with more customer reach, advertising on this platform is currently a must.

However, the timing is critical as well because the advertising space on the platform is shrinking which means that advertising costs have begun to slightly increase and are likely to steadily increase. This increase will only get wider as 2017 proceeds, and the explosion of online business creation continues putting pressure on the advertising platform.

So how do you advertise on Facebook? How do you create the ads? In the next section of this chapter, I'll break down a simple step-by-step review for the beginner advertiser who wants to get into advertising on the platform.

MASSIVE ACTION EXERCISE: Facebook Ads Manager

First things first, you will need to navigate to Facebook Ads Manager in a Chrome browser window and set up your ads account and account pixel. No worries, there are easy tutorials already there to assist with this setup.

Next, go inside the ads manager area by clicking on Create an Ad. This area is organized by three levels: Campaign, Ad Set, and Ad.

Campaign level. An advertising/marketing campaign is where you plan how to connect your audience to your product. Perhaps you've created a webinar, and you want to get them to register for it; or you're selling a product, and you want to run a promotion to achieve sales. You'd name the campaign according to that plan. For example, "webinar registrations for your shiny new course." This is the larger container where everything you do on advertising related to this effort is held within this file.

Ad set. Within the campaign comes a set of targeted ideas to reach the market. For instance, say you're running a promotion for glittery lip gloss. You know you'll need an ad that targets millennial women from 18–

34. But perhaps you want to test another audience set of women from 35–45 to see what traction is there. All of these ad sets targeted to discrete audiences are then housed together in a sub area of the campaign and referred to as the ad set.

Now, certainly, you could target both sets of customers, but you'd need to do so in different language. These different marketing communications in specific language catered to each market set represent the ads you then need to create.

Ah, the ubiquitous Facebook ad. This is the product that contains the custom language that captures the attention and deeper interest in the offer; a custom design or selected graphic to visually convey the emotion you want to express; and most importantly, a call to action. You will want to refer to the next section where I discuss the smart ad template created by the masterful Nicholas Kusmich, a Facebook marketing genius.

The best ads connect the viewer to an emotion right from the start, then the visual draws them nearer, and the call to action takes them home. It is the successful execution of this process—the campaign, ad sets, and the ads—that is anything but simple. It is one of the most excruciating and frustrating parts of doing online marketing. It has, in fact, driven more than a few would-be entrepreneurs back to the loving arms of a corporate day job, and I totally understand the inclination after a while at this.

There are a few areas where there is wide agreement on critical success factors for advertising on Facebook at this point. Use this as your starting point, and you will find success a lot sooner than if you go it alone.

How to Create Facebook Ads

So as not to overwhelm you, I'll again simplify the steps so that they are more easily digested, and you can then focus on the creation process for the campaigns, ad sets, and ads, instead of the technical stuff about how to set it up.

I want to emphasize that success is not in the tech, it's in the spec, if you will. The specifications (specs) are the information pieces that you will need to enter into the pre-formatted sections that the Facebook system prompts will guide you through.

You want to focus your efforts on this specification creation as it will yield 80% of your success. Once you have systematically and consistently yielded the 80%, you can tweak it to yield more success.

Nicholas Kusmich, a well-known and highly regarded Facebook marketing expert based on his high return on investments through his advertising techniques, has provided a smart template. This template simplifies the basic strategy you need to use for the ad copy on all of your ads. Your ad specifications should include all eight pieces.

1. Ask a question that you know will be answered with a deeply emotional yes.

2. Create a connection in the follow-up statements based on the mutually shared experience of that yes answer.
3. Create a sense that time is of the essence so that there should be no delay in taking action—tell them to do it TODAY.
4. Make the irresistible offer of the campaign.
5. Ask them to do something to get it: Download, Book a Call, Sign Up, etc.
6. Place a striking and visually interesting graphic in the middle of the post.
7. Tell them the benefit of the offer—let them know why it will matter to their lives.
8. Add another link to your call to action statement.

NOTES:

_____

_____

_____

_____

_____

_____

_____

_____

_____

_____

_____

_____

_____

_____

_____

_____

_____

Email marketing strategy & best practices

A couple of years ago the rumor spread that email marketing was dead. It's been two years, and I don't know about you, but my inbox is always threatening its storage capacity limits with hundreds of emails added per day. But, yes, times are changing. Email marketing is not dead; it's just different.

The latest craze with Facebook's Messenger application entering the advertising fray portends to be a real game changer. There are now third-party developer apps furiously building automation tools, bots they call them, to help make instant connections with customers, and it's working. Engagement and open rates are currently through the roof with 80%+ open rates on the Messenger notifications. You definitely want to stay tuned and jump in on this trend.

Emailing marketing is not dead, yet. While the Messenger app is new fertile ground and still in its infancy, there are a few email strategies that business owners should be using to improve their business revenue metrics, and we have the data from industry leaders to support them.

One of the leaders in online marketing, HubSpot, is a software developer and marketer of products for inbound marketing and sales. They build their brand through prolific content creation for businesses that need help with their sales and marketing strategies. As an online business owner, this is invaluable because of the wide collection of research content available for free on their site.

In HubSpot's 2017 Marketing Statistics, Trends & Data – The Ultimate List of Marketing Statistics shows the following stats for email click-through rates:

1. 54% of marketers say increasing engagement rate is their top email marketing priority. (Ascend2, 2016)
2. 11 a.m. ET has the highest click-through rate for email sends. (HubSpot, 2015)
3. 15% of marketers surveyed say their company still does not regularly review email opens and clicks; only 23% say they have integrated their website and emails to track what happens after a click. (MarketingProfs, 2016)
4. Email notifications about abandoned carts have a 40.5% open rate. (eMarketer, 2015)
5. As the number of images in an email increases, the click-through rate of the email tends to decrease. (HubSpot, 2014)

On email segmentation, the report reveals that:

1. 42% of marketers do not send targeted email messages; only 4% use layered targeting. (MarketingProfs, 2016)
2. 83% of companies use at least basic segmentation for their emails. (Econsultancy, 2016)
3. The ability to segment email lists and individualize email campaign messaging are the

most effective personalization tactics for 51% and 50% of marketing influencers respectively. (Ascend2, 2016)
4. Segmented and targeted emails generate 58% of all revenue. (The Direct Marketing Association, 2015)

DigitalMarketer.com is the other go-to source for many online business owners who need to stay on top of the fast-changing digital marketing environment. They, too, are prolific content marketers and provide a wealth of free tools on their site.

Ryan Deiss, founder and CEO of DigitalMarketer.com, has also written a best-selling book on the topic called *Invisible Selling Machine*. The book does a great job of organizing the best practices already in play, putting them into a process, and creating a sustainable and winning system in your business.

Deiss captures the essence of the process in what he calls the "5 Phases of Invisible Selling." The phases are the strategic elements of communicating with your customers via email: Indoctrination (introducing yourself and your brand story), Engage (building relationship about their interests), Ascend (welcoming them into the fold and offering more value and ways to help them), Segment (giving them only what they've expressed interest in), and Re-engage/Win Back (moving them from the cool back burner and bringing them back to a warming stage to let them know you're still in their corner).

Example Scenario and Email Sequence

Using our professional editor scenario, how would she go about creating a winning email campaign strategy? The first thing she should do is choose the product line she will launch to her market. Although she needs to choose one to begin with, if she is a multi-passionate entrepreneur, I can guarantee there are many options from which she could choose. But after some deep thinking and alignment with her revenue goals of hitting $10,000 within her first 30 days of business, she decides on the product line for aspiring authors and a full-service community built specifically catering to them.

Based on having determined three different levels of product value, she will need to write an email sequence for each product. Presuming, of course, that she's already written her sales page copy for the product, or has blogged extensively, or maybe has done guest podcast interviews about the product line, and has a few readers on her email list.

The first product will be the lowest cost product but still needs to offer tremendous value. For example, a PDF e-book on self-editing. That product should have a sequence of no more than three to five days of emails. People will become frustrated easily with excessive pitches for what they see as low value (based on price) offers. They demand more attention to the details once the price begins to escalate.

For the first product, she chooses a three-day sequence of emails for readers already on her list, and she segments a five-day sequence for those coming from cold traffic (not already on her list).

The three-day sequence looks like this:

Day 1 Welcome Email & Introduction Email:

Thank You & Welcome! The purpose of this email is to thank them for signing up and downloading your freebie (i.e. a 3-page guide to character development), to provide instructions on where to get the freebie if they haven't downloaded it yet, and to let them know they can ask you any questions because you actually read all of your emails. Make sure to ask them to open it and reply to your email so that you know they got it. Be sure to format your emails in compliance with the CAN-SPAM Act (FTC compliance and allow the users to unsubscribe at the bottom should they want to go).

Indoctrination/Introduction Email. The purpose of this email is to introduce yourself directly so that you start to build on the budding comfort levels established when they decided to opt in to your emails. You will tell them who you are, why you started your business, what unique value you bring to the market, what they will get from you, how often, and what's next (tease them about the product).

Day 2 Second Introduction Email:

This email begins the backstory about the product you mentioned in the last email: what its benefits are and why that should matter to them. Why you think it may solve their problem based on their interest in your lead magnet. You're framing the product as the next logical step once you've already connected them emotionally to the next problem they will have solved. You make the soft sell here and let them know that tomorrow kicks off a buy it now opportunity for them and possibly a bonus.

Day 3 Hard Sell:

The third email is the hard sell of the product. Basically, your sales page in an email with all the bells and whistles laid out, and the compelling reasons they need to make the purchase right now. At the end, you should be laying the ground work for the next product in the series as well.

You will use these same emails with your cold traffic except that on the front end you will spend a couple more days with more of your backstory, maybe sending them to your most popular blog posts, other social media hangouts, etc. Warming them up a bit by showing that you are a real person with a real presence, and they should not worry. Then complete the series the same way as the warm traffic.

The other sequences are built on the same idea. You want to carry the prospect along your sales process while providing them with value and helping them solve problems both big and small. Figure out what makes sense based on your product for each type of client you're hoping to work with.

Creating a winning email marketing campaign in your business can make a huge difference in revenue so getting it right at the outset puts you way ahead of the game. It's even more critical that you have a well-integrated sales process along with this marketing strategy. You need to be able to send people from those email links to a beautiful sales page and shopping cart to buy your stuff. We will dive deeper into sales and marketing funnels in the next chapter.

The next massive action exercise will help you think through and strategize how your own campaign will look. If you're not good at copywriting, or even if you are, you should seek out resources on email copywriting for this part of your business.

MASSIVE ACTION EXERCISE:

- Start writing your backstory copy. This is copy that will be used over and over in many areas of your emails, website, blogs, sales pages, etc. Spend a good deal of time perfecting it to be compelling, succinct, and captivating so they want to hear more from you.
- Think through a great lead magnet (freebie) for your product line. Make sure it has the essential elements of a high-converting lead magnet. Here

are the top 6 from Top Dog Social Media: (1) helps the reader solve a problem/challenge, (2) is very specific, (3) focuses on one big take away, (4) is easy to consume (think checklist or worksheet), (5) is of exceptional value, and (6) builds trust and establishes your expertise.

- Begin outlining your email strategy based on the discussion above. Work from the first moment your prospect meets your lead magnet. At that point, how will you introduce yourself, get to know them better, give them your elevator speech, and find out how you can work together for the rest of your lives? Use the Five Phases of Invisible Selling discussed earlier and begin drafting email sequences based on those goals for your product.

NOTES:

_____

_____

_____

_____

_____

_____

_____

_____

_____

_____

_____

_____

_____

_____

_____

_____

_____

Here are a few golden nuggets for this chapter. If you don't get anything else, get this.

It is said that *almost* everyone (at least in the USA) hates to be sold to. But for the US-based customer, being able to buy stuff is our way of life. It is like the air we breathe. Part of the American Dream. We just need to feel like it was our idea to buy.

Selling happens best when it is invisible to the process. If we just help the customers do what they want to do, which is to buy stuff, there is no need to sell to them.

If we take ourselves out of the way and let the customer and the product/service do their dance, selling is a by-product of that relationship.

What this means is that you must ensure that the product/service you offer is *exactly—and only*—what they already want to buy. If you get this right, when you go to do your Facebook ad targeting and stay the course, you will be hashtag winning in short order.

Don't start advertising until you have set aside cash to gamble with until you figure it all out. It takes time for the system to optimize your pixel code for what you want it to do, and when it looks promising, you'll need to start testing in order to start scaling the most successful ads. Which means you'll need to start spending more and doubling your budgets for new ads.

It's typical that you might get some things wrong out of the gate. But following the guidance I've put in this chapter will decrease your downtime. There are a lot of moving parts to get working together but stay the course. Don't give up and don't turn the ads off too early.

Test only after you've seen something positive happening in the ad metrics consistently, or you start getting sales. You will be extremely frustrated with the process. It's not all on you. It's mostly because you've been left with unrealistic expectations.

If you make an honest reflection of what you're doing— creating and launching a full-fledged business online— you should come to an inflection point where you realize that this is not playing the lottery and owning and operating a business is hard work. It's why entrepreneurs deserve the spoils of their hard work. This is also why there will always be many, many more employees than employers.

You just have to decide who you want to be and resolve to be that guy or gal and don't beat yourself up about which best suits you. Serial entrepreneur that I am, I'm all in. I take the bruises and rub on the salve to live and fight another day and try to bring you along with me by sharing the experience.

Once you get your ads on fire and make consistent connections, you need to make sure you have a high-functioning system in place to continue generating connections, making sales, and processing payments. That's where the sales and marketing funnels come in to play. Check out the next chapter for more on that.

NOTES:

CHAPTER SEVEN

YOU NEED TO FAIL FASTER!

Sales & Marketing Funnel Strategies
Week 7

"Be bold enough to use your voice, brave enough to listen to your heart, and strong enough to live the life you've always imagined."
Unknown

By now if you've followed all the steps, you know:

- your why;
- your ideal client;
- where they hang out;

- what's likely the strongest way to deliver your content to them and what you should create to solve their problems;
- what messaging you need to match your market; and
- how to get your message out via website or blogs, social media advertising, and email marketing.

The next step is to go deep into how you make sales an automatic output of your business. You're setting up a business that has an intrinsic mission to serve others and give as much value as you have. In return for great work and smartly building your business's technology foundation, you should earn all the money you need to continue serving your community.

The business of automating customer acquisition

Automating customer acquisition is the final step in my seven-step framework for multi-passionate entrepreneurs creating online businesses. To do this you need to create your sales and marketing funnel strategy. Deciding on and implementing the necessary technology to run a successful online business is probably the most common problem new entrepreneurs experience when getting started. There are so many choices, most specializing in one particular aspect of a process, and many with stiff learning curves.

A sales funnel simplified

There are three specific aspects of the automated customer acquisition sales process that every business will need regardless of product, service, or industry. Each of these aspects is integrated into what's called a sales funnel. A sales funnel is how online marketers describe the process of taking a prospect from introduction to paid customer.

1. You will need a way to communicate regularly with customers (email auto-responder);
2. A way to showcase your offers and collect email subscribers (sales pages and landing pages); and
3. A way to take orders and process payments (order forms to collect billing information and shopping carts to process credit cards).

The specific steps of the most basic sales funnel process include four major web pages that help move prospects from each phase of your funnel. This basic funnel is also sometimes referred to as a minimum viable funnel for launching new products.

1. The opt in/squeeze/landing page where you provide a little explanation about your freebie (lead magnet) and collect email addresses and other contact information.
2. The thank you page signifying that they've opted in.
3. The sales page containing the details about the offer, including videos and testimonials.

4. The sales confirmation page which provides the receipt and the message for how to access the purchase.

Tools of the Trade

You need a way to pull the funnel process together and seamlessly do business online. First, you need a customer relationship management system (CRM) to handle communications between you and your customers. An email auto-responder is a type of CRM specifically handy in the online marketing world as the communication is typically through automated emails. Automated in the sense that you prepare the emails once in a batch, upload them to the auto-responder, and schedule them to automatically push out to your customers. Very cool concept. I still picture sitting on the beach sipping Mai Tais while thousands of my customers get sweet emails from me.

Next, you need a page builder to create the design of your marketing messages for sales offers as well as for email subscribers to go sign up. Your advertisements announcing your new offers will send your traffic to this page. Along with these email landing pages, you'll need a platform that builds full sales pages where you can design the layout of your sales and marketing messages and collect order form information.

Then, you need a payment processor to accept customer payment and billing information and integrate with merchant processors to take credit card payments. SamCart and any number of other shopping cart solutions all have their pros and cons as every system does. Other options include WooCommerce, BigCommerce, Volusion, Wix, GoDaddy, etc.

Sales Funnel Platforms

There are quite a few different sales funnel platforms around such as Unbounce, Instapage, HubSpot, etc., with many more in development. I'd advise you to do some basic research about the features you need and choose the best one for you at the time based on your current budget. Once you get your business going, you can begin to make choices strategically because of how your business actually works so that you get the most out of the system you choose.

Once you're at a place beyond building an email list, you will want to consider different ways to communicate with your target market about your products. The platform I use and recommend in this framework is the ClickFunnels Etison Suite platform because it outshines its competitors for most businesses hands down.

For example, you can start with a blog post in an ad that sends prospects to your squeeze page where you will obtain their email address, and then on the thank you page, you can easily offer them more value by linking to a sales page for an upcoming webinar on the topic they're interested in from the blog post.

Once on the webinar, you can seamlessly link the webinar attendee to a sales page to purchase an online course to explore the topic more in depth, or even purchase a personal coaching package to indoctrinate the customer in your system. All of these steps can be created in one master funnel structure, within an hour.

The platform gives you the ability to quickly create a sales path to move specific customers through and introduce them to multiple products in your marketing funnel. This is done all while capturing and segmenting your growing email list in Actionetics, a powerful auto-responder fully integrated to handle multiple email sequences and robust tracking of your funnel analytics including open stats and sales conversions.

The Etison Suite also comes with a module for you to build out a full membership site for your business, along with an affiliate program tracker for leveraging other vendors to help sell your products. There are a number of other mini funnels within a master funnel that are deployed at different points in the sales process dependent on product type, customer type, and sales type. For all of this functionality under one software, it's a pretty sweet system and great value for the cost.

More than the cost, it's the savviest all-in-one solution on the market today. The simple to use and highly customizable features make this the go-to platform for any entrepreneur in any space, hands down. You can grow a cool hobby like blogging just for a small tribe all the way up to a mega online business, all while on the same platform.

Having the ability to change your offerings, your methods of message or content delivery, your products, and your ways to gather the tribe as needed means that as a multi-passionate entrepreneur, you can now fit all of your zany ideas onto one platform and create the serial businesses you were born to create. It. Is. Nirvana.

Using a competitor's model to get started: funnel hacking

For those of you who haven't figured out your product yet but still want to get started learning how to make money online while you figure it out, you might consider finding a product that's already winning and modeling it. That way you can study the winning copy and model the sales structure.

In the online world, this is called funnel hacking. You review the presentation of all the sales and marketing materials in a product's purchase process; this means you need to buy said product to see how the business markets to the customer all throughout the funnel.

After you know the full structure, the object is to recreate the structure as closely as possible without stealing it, ensuring all the winning elements are captured in your new funnel providing you with a winning system. Some people struggle with this as they question the method as somehow not ethical. That's because the line between modeling and ripping it off can be difficult to follow without breaching if you're not diligent to do so.

People who are quick to stall and operate out of their fears will not see a way past this. Others will understand they need to make it their own while following a basic pattern of the sales process and using similar appeals to the market already familiar with this type of product. This is the essence of creating alternative products in any market. How many cereals are knockoffs of the Cheerios brand? How many burger joints are there in America alone? Same thing here. Get your burger on.

Creating your own product and funnel

Then there's creating your own product (which once it's a winner, others will funnel hack you as well ... bonus!) and setting it to a sales and marketing funnel. This is likely how most service professionals get started in their online businesses, and it makes sense to do so. Odds are that whatever product you'd want to bring to market is something that you're pretty well versed in and have some passion for. Typically, these same professionals have had a number of years in their careers by this point. They've likely developed or envisioned several solutions for the people they serve.

While I am a seasoned business professional, I was torn on what service to offer due to my multi-passionate nature. Fortunately, when I felt this confusion, I was in a training program for online marketing techniques and strategies developed by Russell Brunson, founder of ClickFunnels.

Brunson delivers this video training session where he dives deep into your business relationship with your customers and the journey on which you set out to take them. The whole process is captured within what's called a value ladder. He defines the value ladder as it relates to online business models: starting with the introduction of the initial low-cost offer for your customer.

From there, the value of your solutions is escalated up the metaphorical ladder structure for the customer to ascend with you incrementally over time.

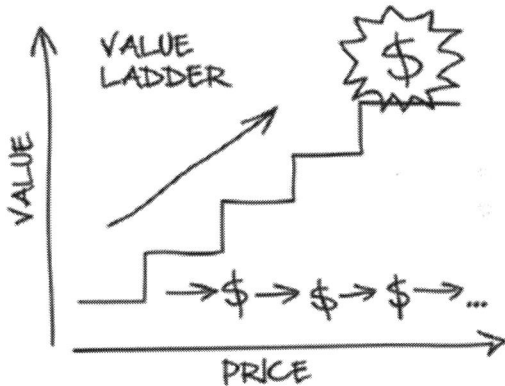

Figure 1 Russell Brunson's Value Ladder Conceptual Graphic

I was able to take all of the ideas I had swimming in my head and overlay them on this value ladder concept as my online business model. It's a fairly organized way to look at all of the solutions you might want to provide the folks you serve. It will help you to consider pricing the value of the solution and where it fits within the relationship and where you are on the ladder.

You're now determining a marketing strategy to reach your cold (people completely unaware of you), warm (prospects who have an awareness of the problem you solve), and hot (customers who know you and your product) traffic leads and build out your funnel. There are a few foundational funnels that savvy internet marketers like Russell Brunson, Todd Brown, and a host of others have shown us work through their testing and validating through the years.

The top five typical funnels used by online businesses:

These are the top five funnels used in most online businesses today.

1. Free plus shipping/handling book funnel (a great way to introduce yourself and build credibility)
2. Self-liquidating offer funnel (this pays for your costs to acquire customers)
3. Continuity funnel (for monthly membership programs)
4. Sales webinar funnel (for middle-cost products/services ranging from $297–1,497)
5. High ticket application funnel (for coaching/consulting programs)

Depending on your business model and the type of products or services you offer, there are many options for you to use in creating your marketing plan. The best way I've found is to take an objective and unattached assessment of the options, understand how these funnels are used and for what audiences they've worked well, and then go from there.

MASSIVE ACTION EXERCISE:

- Think about your product opportunities and create a value ladder for your business.
- Select the platform to host your funnel. To try ClickFunnels Free for 14 days, go to http://bit.ly/2vb315H. This is my affiliate link, so I may earn a small amount from your purchase at no cost to you. You will pay the same amount to ClickFunnels whether you use my link or anyone else's. I do offer to support anyone using my affiliate link with setting up their first funnel at no charge. Win-win.
- Then construct the funnel to address one of those offers in your value ladder. Create the offers and incorporate the sales copy into the funnel software you're using.
- Create your ads, and give it a whirl!
- Create your automated emails based on the tips given in the last chapter.
- Analyze the results (review your system for how many emails were opened, and how many sales occurred, etc.) and drop me an email to let me know how it's going!

NOTES:

The best approach to all of this is that you are testing your hypothesis of what you think will work. So remain detached from all outcomes. Even once you've landed on the winner, remain detached from that outcome and focus on serving the people who have come to you for help.

It is in serving people that all other wisdom about how to do it better will develop. This will also serve your sanity because the effort won't drag you down into an abyss of feeling like a loser because your campaign isn't working as you want it to.

Just unplug from those thoughts and always remember it's not about you. It's about the universe's way of delivering you to exactly where you're meant to be to serve who you're meant to serve. God will take care of the rest, my friends!

THE WRAP UP

We've now covered the most critical aspects of growing your successful online business. So, let's piece this all together from the top.

In chapter one, you examined how to go mining through your life to find your *why*. Creating a successful online business is complicated, time consuming, and full of little failures that serve to train you along the way, so you need your "why" to guide you.

Finding your "why" is likely just as hard or harder than the worst personal or professional development experience you've ever endeavored to undertake. Tenacity, persistence, and consistency are all required skill sets to reach any level of success online.

You uncovered your gifts and passions, pulling them to the forefront of your mind to guide you. This is your "why"—your daily reason for every step you need to take to create the business and life you want.

Then in chapter two, you examined who it is you want to serve, recognizing that although it sounds great at first, "everyone" is not your target market. You homed in on the exact ideal client or customer you're meant to serve.

It should be noted here that if you're a multi-passionate, you are meant to serve more than one group of people. Following my framework will help you to figure out how to go deep and determine how to assimilate your skills and reach more than one group with those same skills. Create something new.

Start where you need to start. Just start and don't make excuses for inaction. Serve someone outside of yourself. The desire has to come from within you. No guru has that answer for you.

I believe God gifts us with skills he needs us to develop from season to season. It's why I think we come across different people at seemingly random times in our lives and can't immediately discern why the connection happened, especially if it's not a long-lasting connection. Use that seasonality to flavor what you come up with.

In chapter three, you learned how to determine where your prospects hang out online and steps to create your online profiles so that you can reach your ideal clients.

In chapter four, you learned how to create the product or service your ideal customer wants and which vehicle to use to deliver the product. After you've politely asked and received the feedback within your survey structure, you can drill down a bit to see how they are connecting or not connecting with your product or products similar to yours.

Are your customers more likely to want video lessons or weekly coaching calls on Zoom, for instance? Understanding what your competitors are already providing and researching what the students are saying about those products can clue you in to what's missing in the marketplace. This is a great way to develop stand out products that serve your market.

In chapter five, you learned how to match your messages to your market. We discussed how you need to differentiate your product from competition in a way that resonates with your market. Whether the prospects are from cold, warm, or hot traffic makes a real difference in how you address them.

The chapter six discussion around online business marketing strategies puts into perspective the use of the top three strategies in play today: website/blog; top social media advertising platforms like Facebook and Instagram; and effectively using email marketing campaigns.

YouTube is in the process of making a serious play to capture more of this marketplace by expanding its features and offerings to make it easier and more compelling for online businesses to put content on their search engine platform.

I look forward to working more with YouTube in the coming months and will have updates for those folks on my email list, so make sure you're on it. Make sure you sign up to join me at www.facebook.com/onlinebizhackers.

Finally, in chapter seven we discuss bringing it all together for the purpose of providing the valuable products and services your customers need. From communicating with them via automated emails to helping them ascend through your value ladder of offerings, using an automated sales and marketing funnel platform like ClickFunnels is the smart strategy.

CONCLUSION

Around the time I was introduced to the imposter syndrome concept, I ran smack dab into powerful marketing by Todd Herman and his 90 Day Year business coaching program. In a word, arresting. I stopped in my tracks on all levels.

Now, I'm not one who just throws around praise for praise sake. Herman has this training video series as part of the pre-launch for his semiannual program, and it is stunning in its elegant simplicity. Totally my kind of thing. Not full of fluff, well executed, and a solid connection to multiple pain points for entrepreneurs of all industries.

He developed this concept of the Oww™ and Wow™ brain where in the former you are drawn to seeing the events of your life through a negative and pessimistic prism, and through the latter, it's much more positive and optimistic, allowing you to push through faster to the end goals you've set. Bouncing back from all the setbacks makes the difference between quitters and winners. That was breathtaking for me at that moment.

I trapped myself and all of my progress into an Oww mindset, stuck and ineffective. Hearing Herman describe this concept and showing these examples was like a gut punch. Hard. All the thoughts I had simmering on the back burner boiled over.

It was only me, my decisions, that were holding me back. I had been a very accomplished person by any standard in this tough life and could be again in anything I choose. I needed to choose it. Then go do it. Are you in the same situation? Do you need to just be the decider in chief of your own life? Give yourself permission to Get S@#!t Done. Now THAT will change your life!

Finally, I wrote this book as a companion to my concierge business service so that more people can get started on their own journey with an actionable guide to help along the way. It's full of golden nuggets that have helped me and others to reach for our dreams.

If any of what you've read has resonated with you, I invite you to join me on this mission to create the life of your dreams through your business success.

The world awaits your gift ...

See you on the other side.

ABOUT THE AUTHOR

Juanita Renee Jones, a 20+ year veteran project management consultant, took her local consulting business online last year, and the experience awakened a serial online entrepreneur.

Using entrepreneurship as the vehicle, Juanita wants to inspire people to do what they love and use their life to serve others with the greatest impact possible.

In the local Detroit area, she helps investors take their real estate assets from distressed to well-dressed.

To find out more about Juanita and to inquire how you can work with her on your business, go to www.juanitareneejones.com. You can find her on social media at www.facebook.com/onlinebizhackers; Instagram @onlinebizhackers.

Juanita lives and works in her native hometown of Detroit, Michigan.

One More Question? Could you use an Entrepreneur's Treasure Chest?

Hi, my name is Juanita Renee Jones and I run a business concierge service and online training business on the Internet.

In the next few minutes, you are going to discover how Entrepreneurs from all over the world get their business running as profitably as possible...simply by finding the most efficient and automated way to do everything.

I've collaborated with other experts and we've put together a list of **Freebies, Books, and Special Offers** that will shave hundreds of hours off of your business set up time.

I don't know about you, but time is my most valuable asset! Here's what's included...

- **Business Foundation Hacks and Offers** - Like Bookkeeping, Legal Resources, and Website Deals
- **Productivity** - Like Project Management Tools, Surveys, Schedulers, Polls, Storage, and Passwords
- **Marketing** - Like Email Freebies, Sales Funnel Hacks, Social Media Resources, + Copywriting Swipe Files
- **Design + Branding** - Like Images, Logos, Stock Photos, Color Inspiration, and Design Elements and Freebies

Just click here to get your freebies!

http://bit.ly/2hA8Rui

WAIT! DON'T GO! HEAR MY PLEA!

Review Me!

Graphic By: CC Hogan

THANK YOU, THANK YOU, THANK YOU!

Thank you for purchasing, downloading, and reading my book. As an indie author and self-publisher, it is very rewarding to work on books I know impact my readers' lives. But because I don't have the big budget of the mainstream publishers, it is more important that I ask for your help in reviewing the book. Your review will help me to continue to meet your needs and to serve you with future books.

If you feel that my work has helped you, please **go over to the REVIEW section on Amazon** or wherever you bought this book and drop me a quick line to let me know about any insights and value you gained from the book.

SELF-PUBLISHING
SCHOOL

NOW IT'S YOUR TURN

Discover the EXACT 3-step blueprint you need to become a bestselling author in 3 months.

Self-Publishing School helped me, and now I want them to help you with this FREE WEBINAR!

Even if you're busy, bad at writing, or don't know where to start, you CAN write a bestseller and build your best life.

With tools and experience across a variety niches and professions, Self-Publishing School is the <u>only</u> resource you need to take your book to the finish line!

DON'T WAIT

Watch this FREE WEBINAR now, and
Say "YES" to becoming a bestseller:

http://bit.ly/2rSCwD0

Made in the USA
Columbia, SC
26 January 2019